SHIKATAGANAI
IT CAN'T BE HELPED

The MORISAWA STORY

INCLUDING MEMOIRS AND THE
STORY OF OUR INTERNMENT

By Sumi Kinoshita

Produced by:

FriesenPress

Suite 300 – 852 Fort Street

Victoria, BC, Canada V8W 1H8

www.friesenpress.com

Distributed to the trade by The Ingram Book Company

Table of Contents

I dedicate this to my family and extended family.

In memory of our late
Parents, Kanekichi and Naoye Morisawa;
Sister Diana Iwata;
Brothers Allan Morisawa, George Morisawa
And my husband Matsu Kinoshita.

Acknowledgements

I give many thanks to my siblings David, Kenneth, Amy and late brother George for their contributions of their internment memories and summary of their lives "after the farm." I am grateful for my late sister Diane's "voice" through Ed Suguro of the Northwest News in Seattle in his newspaper article written many years ago. I would like to thank my late mother, Naoye, for leaving us a personal written account of her childhood interviewed by my sister-in-law Taeko Morisawa and my Auntie Lily for her contributions to my story. I am grateful to Cousin Sandi Sasaki's help in formatting, editing and giving me so much invaluable help as I first started to write. To Jean Manky for the hours spent editing I give a wholehearted thank you, and to her husband Brian for scanning photos. Thank you to my son- in- law David Wood and my daughter Karen Wood for so much help with editing, technical details and steering me in the right direction. Finally, to many others like Ken I., Anne K., Elaine S., Suzy M., Roger S. and Maria R., I give thanks for their help, support and encouragement in keeping this story alive.

Preface

In 2009, preparing for our second family reunion which would take place in Castlegar, BC, we decided to visit the sites where my family and other Japanese Canadians were interned during the second world war. We wanted to share our memories with our children and grandchildren. Recording our memories aroused my curiosity as I wondered what actually happened before, during and after the war. With these experiences, the beginning of my story was born.

Using these memories as a starting point, I then added my Auntie Lily's and my siblings' memories about the internment years, and my parents' early lives in Canada based on the oral and written accounts left for us. I've included a historical background of the Japanese Canadians and racism in Canada, the pre and postwar resettling experiences of my family and updates of my families' lives.

Finally, I took the liberty to add some very personal afterthoughts. A determination to tell the whole story for my grandchildren and future generations has overcome my fears of writing about this very dark period in Canadian history. My story is just one of many by former evacuees who have shared their internment experience.

Beginnings

New Country, New Adventures

Like many immigrants first arriving in a new country, my parents struggled to make a living. Economic hardships and racial tensions compounded their difficulties.

The first Japanese settler in Canada was 19-year-old Manzo Nagano who likely jumped ship in New Westminster in 1877 before making his home in Victoria, BC. Hearing of Manzo's successes, first as a pioneer and later as an entrepreneur, others from all over Japan began to follow.[1]

Since the mid-1700s British Columbia was settled by mainly British and European immigrants, and the intention was to keep British Columbia as a British colony. Due to the need for laborers, British Columbia was unable to exclude the new settlers from entering the country, but the early BC settlers being proud

1 Historical information is drawn from: N. Rochelle Yamagishi, *Japanese Canadian Journey,* The Nakagawa Story, (Victoria, BC: Trafford Publishing, 2010); Pamela Hickman & Masako Fukawa, *Righting Canada's Wrongs: Japanese Canadian Internment in the Second World War,* (Toronto: James Lorimer & Company Ltd., 2011)and Rose Murakami, *Ganbaru: the Murakami Family of Salt Spring Island,* (Salt Spring Island, BC: Japanese Garden Society of Salt Spring Island,1992

of their British and European origins sought to exclude the new immigrants from society. These new immigrants, mainly Chinese, Indo Canadians and Japanese were excluded for their different language, appearance and actions.

On arrival in Canada, the immigrants were soon met with great disappointment. Paid far less than Caucasians and unable to find decent housing, the new immigrants struggled in a climate of racism. Although many became homesick for Japan, they found themselves unable to make enough money to return. Being illiterate in English and living in rundown housing forced a stronger grouping together and support for one another as they faced an increasingly hostile society. Many Japanese immigrants became skilled in their work, causing even more racial tension as British and European Canadians became fearful of losing their jobs and being replaced by the lower paid, industrious immigrants.

As with most immigrants there was a tendency for them to stay together for support, socializing and sharing mutual interests. Culturally, the Japanese believed in a strong sense of community, supporting one another and helping one another. This forced stronger grouping together. This increased the accusations that the Japanese were unable to assimilate into Canadian society.

Entry into various professions required citizens to be on the voter's list, but laws were passed which denied the new immigrants the right to vote. Therefore, the new immigrants were excluded from many occupations such as civil service, law, pharmacy and medicine, to name a few. The fact that they had become Canadian citizens failed to make a difference.

The new immigrants were prohibited from buying crown land. Purchasing land from a willing landowner was the only way they could own property. Also, the Japanese Canadian children whose parents could not afford to buy property (and most couldn't) were not allowed to attend public school.

For most of the 1800's, Japan prohibited its citizens from travelling abroad, but the Meiji Restoration, Japan's new government in 1868, allowed and even encouraged the Japanese people to leave the country. Many went to Hawaii to work on sugar plantations. Some moved to New Caledonia, Australia, Fiji and various other places in the United States.

Soon the small trickle of immigrants coming to Canada became a steady flow of predominantly young, single Japanese males. Eventually a steamship carrying these immigrants began regularly leaving Yokohama, Japan and arriving in Vancouver, British Columbia.

The little town of Steveston became the second largest Japanese settlement in BC next to Japan Town in Vancouver. Some of the immigrants worked in the mines while others worked in sawmills. The majority of the early arrivals continued the work they were accustomed to in their homeland, mainly fishing and farming. The young men were poor but hard working and adventurous, expecting to find good jobs and return home richly dressed with fortunes jingling in their pockets. Lured by contractors promising exaggerated and favorable housing conditions, most immigrants arrived with borrowed money.

My maternal grandfather, Inosuke Nakata, escaping the crushing poverty in Japan where there was a deep divide between the wealthy and the poor, probably arrived in this first wave of settlers in the late 1890s and early 1900s. He settled in the town of Steveston, BC. He joined the fishing community and later arranged for a wife to come from Japan.

Fearing that the Japanese were going to dominate the fishing industry, the provincial government reduced the number of fishing permits allowed. Forbidden from joining the BC Fisherman's Union, the Japanese were forced to form their own union. By 1919, the BC Fisherman's Union, with the support of

BC politicians, successfully lobbied the Federal Government to eliminate almost half of Japanese fisherman's permits.

Although the cheap labor provided by the Japanese immigrants was needed, the Caucasian community was unwilling to allow these perceived "lower class" people to assimilate among them. They were accused of being inassimilable due to their race, color and culture which was deemed inferior to the British way of life.

In early September 1907, the Asiatic Exclusion League organized a massive anti-Asiatic parade, complete with a brass band. As one speaker after another denounced the Oriental menace and the need to put a stop to Asian immigration, the crowd of 9,000 quickly became riotous and began marching into Chinatown and Japan Town, breaking windows and destroying property.

Soon Ottawa joined forces to deal with "the Oriental problem." The government tried making life miserable for the Japanese, hoping they would return to Japan. This only made the Japanese community stronger and more determined to prove their loyalty to Canada. It also forced them into further segregation from the rest of the population. Creatively forming their own communities by opening cafes, grocery stores, bakeries, cleaners and hardware stores they tried to provide for their own socioeconomic needs. For example, the fishing town of Steveston, BC was one of these communities that had its own Japanese schools, churches and businesses to meet their own needs.

Following the 1907 anti-Asian riot until approximately 1924, Japanese immigrants to Canada were limited to 400 men (no women) per year. Therefore, a picture bride system *shashin kekkon* was instituted[2]. This was a form of traditional matchmaking using photographs, and couples could be married by proxy i.e.,

2 Information, courtesy Nikkei National Museum, Burnaby, BC; Japanese Canadian Journey, N. Rochelle Yamagishi, Trafford Publishing, Victoria, BC. 2010. Righting Canada's Wrongs: Japanese Canadian Internment in the Second

the prospective bride could be married in Japan in the absence of the bridegroom. The husbands only had to enter the names of their brides into their family registry in Japan. Thus the men and women became legally married no matter where they lived.

Forced to stay in Canada due to economic hardship, many single males longing for marriage sent photos of themselves (usually a younger, more handsome picture of themselves or, at least, one in which they dressed up wearing a borrowed suit) home to relatives in Japan hoping to attract potential wives and take advantage of the *shaskin kekkon*. Considering the family background, age and wealth, families in Japan with the help of a *go-between* tried to find suitable matches for the men, usually from the same village in Japan. In return, prospective brides sent their own photos back to Canada. They sometimes sent a picture of their sister or friend instead, hoping to impress their intended.

My maternal grandmother, Haruye (nee Inabe) Nakata was one of those picture brides. She married my grandfather, Inosuke Nakata and settled in Steveston B.C.

Stories are told of these picture brides being shocked on arrival when meeting their future husbands for the first time. Some of the men did not look anything like the photos that they sent nor did the lifestyle match the description the men had given. In turn, many men failed to recognize their brides who didn't match their pictures.

In fact, my grandfather's brother had intended to marry my grandmother- Haruye Inabe, but my grandfather wanting to marry her himself, persuaded his brother to let him do so.

When the couples were eventually matched with one another, in spite of disappointment, they continued in their marriages in the

---

World War: Pamela Hickman and Masako Fukawa, James Lorimer &Company Ltd., Publishers, Toronto, 2010 spirit of *shikata ga nai* (it can't be helped i.e. one's fate is beyond one's personal control), and courage, strength and *gambaru* (perseverance) in the Japanese way. There were rare stories of love at first sight.

Other single males who had enough money returned to Japan to bring back wives arranged for them by a *baishakunin* (go-between). Meanwhile, married men sent for their wives and families and settled into their new surroundings and growing Japanese communities.

My father Kanekichi Morisawa (his father's last name was spelled Morizawa) immigrated to Canada in 1919 as a single male with borrowed money. By 1931 he had enough money to return to Japan to look for a wife. A go-between arranged for him to meet my mother, Naoye Nakata, a second generation Canadian living in Japan, who was ready to return to Canada. My paternal grandparents, Seihechi and Toku (nee Washita) Morizawa remained in Japan.

By 1938, the BC legislature set up a review board to investigate charges of illegal Japanese entry into Canada[3]. As a result all people of Japanese ancestry were required to carry identification cards. The Japanese language schools were closed. The review board proposed that the Japanese be sent to other provinces. In fact, in 1938, Lt. Col. Macgregor McIntosh, Conservative Member of Parliament, recommended the "repatriation" of Japanese residents to Japan, regardless of their citizenship. That event actually took place in 1945 when 4,000 Japanese Canadians "chose" to be repatriated in obedience to the law, "go east of the Rockies or be repatriated to Japan". In 1947 Prime Minister Mackenzie King finally revoked the law.

....

3 Ganbaru: the Murakami Family of Saltspring Island by Rose Murakami, Japanese Garden Society of Salt Spring Island- 1992

As Canada entered the war in Europe and as young men were desperately needed to serve in the military, many Japanese Canadian young males, trying to prove their loyalty to Canada, attempted to enlist in the military and were refused[4]. Long before Japan attacked Pearl Harbor and Canada entered the war against Japan, racism had already spread out its poisonous, ugly tentacles against the Japanese.

Like many immigrants to Canada, our parents were simply trying to make a living to support their growing family. It is against this background that my family's story is told.

---

4 Righting Canada's Wrongs: Japanese Canadian Internment in the Second World War; Pamela Hickman and Masako Fukawa, James Lorimer & Company Ltd., Publishers Toronto.

My Mother

Naoye Nakata

My mother took much delight in telling stories about her childhood, her brief life and romance in Japan and her life after returning to Canada. As difficult as her life was, especially in Kelowna, she still wanted us to be informed and made sure there was a written account left for us. The oral and written accounts are woven together in this story.

My maternal grandparents, Inosuke and Haruye Nakata, settled in the fishing town of Steveston, BC on arrival in Canada in the early 1900s. My mother, Naoye Nakata, the eldest of six children (Naoye, Kimiye, Soichi, Takeo, Yoshio and Tomiye), was born on November 6, 1908 in Steveston BC.

Her father's favorite, my mother as a child was a curious mischievous, headstrong firstborn child. My grandmother had difficulty controlling and disciplining my mother. Consequently, her childhood was a combination of being spoiled by my grandfather and frequently disciplined by my grandmother. My mother admitted to being both a brat and the neighborhood bully.

Along one of the large, deep ditches lining the Steveston roads was my mother's house. It was one of seven connected by a common roof. She was told to never go near the ditch. Knowing there was fish in the water, my mother secretly found a net and rod and tried her hand at fishing. As she cast her rod while standing on a plank crossing the ditch, the line snagged a pole. She lost her balance and fell headfirst into the trench. Though covered with mud and slime, my mother was fortunate the water was shallow. Grateful that my mother was rescued by a Chinese man who took her home, my grandmother was furious with her daughter, the neighborhood mischief maker.

My mother punched kids she didn't like as they passed her house going to school. One day at school, feeling resentful towards another girl showing off her beautiful, white silk blouse, my mother got a pen and scribbled on the back of the lovely blouse. This warranted a spanking from my grandmother when she eventually found out, but my grandfather said nothing.

One day she decided to sneak some of the tobacco she had seen her father chew while he worked on his fishing boat. My mother began eating a sizeable amount that she had found, and it wasn't long before she became sicker than a dog later making all of her hair fall out. Later, the doctor at the hospital took hold of her slipper and gave her a sound spanking. Once again, my grandmother was furious with her while my grandfather said nothing.

My mother enjoyed watching my grandfather and the men work on the boat. While the men were on their tea break, my mother decided to experiment with an intriguing tool that made holes. Having the time of her life, she started drilling holes in her dad's boat. Upon discovery, rather than admonishing his child, my grandfather got to work repairing the damage, mumbling, "Shikataganai, she would have made a dandy son."

My mother remembered getting ahold of her father's rifle. My grandfather, who enjoyed duck hunting, told my mother never to touch that rifle as it was too dangerous for a child. When no one was looking she picked up the rifle and aimed it at a chicken. Much to her delight and satisfaction the bullet hit the target and the chicken keeled over. Again my grandmother was furious while my grandfather said nothing.

At the age of ten, my mother was taken to Japan with her siblings. My grandfather remained in Steveston while my grandmother, expecting another child, needed to care for her mother-in-law who was not well. My mother remained a *yancha* (mischievous one) and a tomboy but no longer had my grandfather to run to when she was in trouble with my grandmother. The month long journey by boat to Japan was difficult, making most of the family seasick. While on the boat, my mother had the task of babysitting her youngest brother, Yoshio. My grandmother was pleased as she watched her oldest finally take on some responsibility.

Soon after arriving in Japan, Tomiye, my mother's youngest sister, was born. To assist my grandmother, my mother's prime responsibility was to care for her two year old brother Yoshio. One day when she was told to take Yoshio outside, he struggled and fought as my mother tried to strap him on her back. He didn't want to go outside. As a result of all his wriggling, Yoshio fell backwards into the pond behind him. My mother, too afraid to tell my grandmother about the incident, went to a neighbour for help. Together they washed the mud off the little boy. Two year old Yoshio soon got very quiet and died shortly after. When they shaved his head to prepare the body for burial, a huge bruise was found on his head. Apparently he died of a massive head injury. I have no other details about this incident, but I remember how terribly sad my mother was as she later recounted this tragedy to us.

As my mother became a teenager, my grandmother and great grandmother decided to hire my mother out as a *Hako* (a babysitter and housemaid). Young ladies from poorer families often worked in wealthy homes without pay to learn to behave in ladylike ways. My mother's first job was caring for several young girls whose parents worked in a garment factory. By the time she reached 18 years of age, she had blossomed into an attractive young woman. She later found work as a housemaid in the home of a bachelor doctor who lived with his mother. My mother's hard work and thriftiness impressed the doctor's mother who thought, "What a fitting bride she would make for my son." My mother was not interested because a go-between had already introduced her to a man she liked very much. She had promised this boyfriend, the man of her dreams that she would wait for him until he came back from the military. Though not formally engaged, he had told her, "Don't marry anyone else."

One day, elated at the news that Kiyoshi, her boyfriend, had returned, my mother got the shock of her life when she found out that he was already married with children. Injured in the military, he had been hospitalized and had fallen in love with his nurse. No one, not even the go-between, had prepared my mother for the devastating news that he had married another woman. Brokenhearted and humiliated, the only thing my mother wanted to do was to get away from Japan.

As was the custom, a go-between arranged for my mother to meet a so-called business man (it was not unusual for prospective grooms to exaggerate their social positions) from Canada who was looking for a wife. Realizing this could be a way to return to her native home and join her family who had preceded her back to Canada, my mother agreed to meet this man who was from the same village, Mio Mura, as she. One thing led to another, and my mother eventually married Kanekichi Morisawa in Wakayama province, Japan in 1931.

My Father

Kanekichi Morisawa

Whereas my mother was born and lived her first 10 years in Canada before going to Japan, my father was born and raised in Japan and came to Canada in his early twenties. My mother was the eldest in her family, my father the youngest in his. They were opposites in temperament and character.

My father, Kanekichi Morisawa, was born in Mio Mura, a picturesque fishing village in the province of Wakayama, August 31, 1898. He was the youngest of six children (Ichitaro, Iwa Matsuno, Toki Tamashiro, Tatsu Osawa, Kinosuke (changed last name to Miyashita) and Kanekichi) born to Seihechi and Toku (nee Washita) Morizawa in Japan.

My father's story of his childhood is sketchy, but history tells us there was much poverty in Japan at the time. My father did tell us how he and his siblings helped the family earn a living by diving for seaweed, fish and abalone and selling them at the markets.

Because my grandfather, Seihichi Morizawa, passed away in Japan and because my father wanted to help the family, he immigrated to Canada circa 1919. He wanted to seek a better life and to send money back to his family in Japan. Promising to reimburse my grandmother for the money she paid for his one-way ticket, my father sailed to Canada. Three of his siblings emigrated to and settled in California before the federal ban on Japanese immigration was implemented there. One of his sisters, Tatsu and her husband eventually worked in a logging camp in Vancouver, Washington. After being interned during the war, they returned to Japan when the war was over.

Another sister Toki, married to her alcoholic husband Mr. Tamaki, settled in Kelowna, BC. Later separating from her husband, she moved to Victoria, BC and eventually married Mr. Tamashiro who worked as a cook on a cable ship. They lived in New Denver, BC during the war and moved out east to Port Arthur, Ont., after the war. After her husband died, Toki returned to Japan where she spent her last days.

My father arrived as most of the other Japanese immigrants–a single male with very little money in his pocket and illiterate in English. He arrived in Canada with a man name Mr. Tamaki who was either a cousin or just a friend. (Information is sketchy according to my brother David) Soon after his arrival in Canada, my father worked as a laborer in sawmills and fishing plants. With his meager earnings, he tried running a dry goods store somewhere along Helmcken St. in Vancouver. When that didn't succeed, he and Mr. Tamaki tried managing a pig farm on rented land where the Oakridge Shopping Centre now stands. Having an alcoholic partner who drank up most of the profits didn't help their economic status. My father later went to Toronto and worked as a houseboy for the owner of the MacMillan Publishing Company. Mrs. MacMillan taught him some English and shorthand. With limited English and business skills, my father was unable to find sufficient work and enough money to reimburse his mother's loan in Japan. By this time, he realized that he wouldn't be returning to Japan to live as he had hoped. Adjusting to life in Canada was difficult and disappointing due to the frustrations of his failed attempts at running businesses and poor communication skills.

Also by this time the deep roots of racism had also taken hold in the province.

However, by the time my father turned 31 years of age, he had saved enough money to return to his native village of Mio Mura, Wakayama province in Japan to look for a wife. With the help of a go-between, he was introduced to Naoye Nakata, a Nisei (second generation Canadian born in Canada) in Mio Mura who was ready to return to Canada. They were married on Feb. 5, 1931 and came to Kelowna, B.C. to start their married life.

The Shed

Kelowna, BC

My mother and father started out as newlyweds in Kelowna, B.C. during dire economic times. It was in the middle of the depression and work was hard to find. My father rented the shed on the Bowman Ranch as their home. He and my mother crop shared with Mr. and Mrs. Bowman.

My mother recounted many stories of life on the Bowman Ranch. What a shock it was for her to be living in a shed and farming at a time when crops were difficult to sell. Such a lifestyle was not what she expected. As they crop shared tomatoes, onions and cantaloupes with the owners of the ranch, many times crops taken to market would return unsold and the produce would have to be dumped in the orchard. It was an extremely difficult and disheartening experience. She ate so many cantaloupes; she couldn't face eating another one for the rest of her life.

My mother recalled how often tears would stream down her face mixed with the sweat running down her brow as she leaned on the hoe, weary from another day of toil in the hot Okanagan sun. She would hear the train rumbling down the track, blowing its whistle until it became a faint echo. She longed to be on that train and be carried away from her present misery.

My mother often wondered how her life took such a turn. How could she have known they would find themselves in the middle of the Great Depression? How could she have known my father was not really a business man but one who had only dabbled in some business attempts? Without family or friends around to talk to, she found adjusting to married life very difficult. She had such great hopes of starting a new life back in her native Canada. She had never farmed or even gardened before and she never thought she would have to touch dirt as a businessman's wife. Now, here she was a poor farmer's wife feeling trapped and living in a shed on an orchard. Many times my mother dreamed of what life would have been like had she been able to marry her first love and stay in Japan.

My mother remembered being a free spirit in Steveston and often thought of her happy childhood there. She felt remorse for the pain and frustration her rebelliousness had caused her mother and for the unkind ways she treated her fellow students at school and in the neighborhood.

When my grandmother, who lived on Vancouver Island, became aware of my mother's difficulties in Kelowna, she sent a letter offering a way to rescue her from her predicament. My mother, who was proud and determined to stick it out, tore up the letter without showing it to my father who would've been upset and humiliated at such a letter.

My mother's firstborn, Diana, arrived on March 24, 1932. When my mother's contractions started at home, my parents had no vehicle to get my mother to the hospital. My father called on a neighbor friend, Mrs. Booth, for help. With an instruction book in hand, Mrs. Booth successfully delivered my parent's first child, Diana Kiyono (known to our family as "Diane"). She slathered the premature baby with lard and kept her warm near the stove.

When their first son, David Tokudo, was born at the Kelowna General Hospital, my mother was grateful for the milkman who took her to hospital in his truck. Kenneth Moritsugu, their third child, was also born at the hospital another year later.

My mother, with sadness in her voice, related how often she had to leave the children locked in the shed alone wondering if they were okay, as she and my father worked from dawn to dusk, coming home only to feed the children. When they did take the children to the field they were taken in a box. As the babies napped, the box was covered with branches to protect them from the eagles flying overhead who might snatch them.

One day while my parents worked alone out in the field, their two little ones came toddling towards them. How in the world did Diane and David get out of that shed and cross over on that plank that bridged the creek? It was a mystery my parents were never able to figure out. Another time the children were left with cornflakes to eat for lunch. When my parents came home, they found the cornflakes mixed with feces finger-painted all over the floor, the wall and the children's bodies. Then there was the day they came home to five dozen eggs smashed all over the floor with the children slipping and sliding through them. Too tired to even think of cleaning up the mess or cooking supper, they could only laugh at the scene.

My parents were ill- prepared for the difficulties of starting life in Canada as newlyweds and the task of facing the challenges which lay ahead. Adjusting to married life, working on an orchard and living in a shed raising small children in the midst of the Depression was not what they had expected. Little did my mother know how many times she would rely upon her childhood spunkiness, curiosity, and determination to overcome all of her challenges. Like others, my mother and father were caught in the middle of a worldwide recession.

3217 Shelly St.

Victoria, BC

My paternal Aunt Toki moved to Victoria, BC alone and married Mr. Tamashiro. They persuaded my parents to join them. To escape the hard life in Kelowna, my parents moved to Victoria, BC in 1935 with their three small children- Diane, David and Ken. This move brought about some positive changes for them. My maternal grandmother and my mothers' siblings were by then living in Ucluelet on the West Coast of Vancouver Island. My maternal Uncle Soichi was a fisherman and was married to my Auntie Kimi; they had two children. Her youngest sister, my maternal Auntie Lily, single, worked in a cannery. Another maternal Auntie Kimiye was married to Shuzo Tsubota, had four children and lived in Port Alberni. They were able to give help and support to my parents.

My parents purchased a small one acre piece of property on which they built their first house and settled down to raise their family. Their new address became 3217 Shelley Street.

1985 - Courtesy Private Collection - Amy Chan, George Morisawa,
Sumi Kinoshita visits old Victoria house (now renovated).

My mother said, "Dad and I built the house together. The foundation was mainly rocks picked up by Diane and David. Together we mixed the rocks and cement in the wheelbarrow. The house had no insulation and no ceiling — just rafters. The floor was so drafty the carpet lifted whenever it was windy out and everyone helped hold it down." We as children gleefully jumped on the carpet to hold it down as it buckled up here and there whenever the wind blew through the basement and up through the living room floor. As rustic as the house was my parents must have felt like they were living in a castle after living in such a humble shed in Kelowna.

My mother explained how they bought 20 chickens and 30 rabbits to raise for food. One day the rabbits escaped when someone forgot to close the door of the rabbit cage. One can only imagine the commotion it caused with the rabbits scampering about everywhere. My father was furious as we ran around trying to catch as many rabbits as possible. We did manage to save a few.

Most escaped and made their home in the Chavez Creek bank. Did they ever multiply in their new found home and freedom!

In order to feed their family which by now had grown to six, my parents raised cauliflower, carrots, beets, scarlet runners, lettuce and tomatoes to earn extra money. My father spaded the garden causing holes in his boots from the constant digging. Not able to afford new ones, he wrapped gunny sacks around his boots to make do while he continued digging.

During the summer my father (known as "Kane-san") worked on an ocean-going cable ship with my uncle, Mr. Tamashiro, the chief cook on the ship. This was the way my father learned some cooking skills which held him in good stead in later years. When my father was away, a friend kindly took the vegetables into town to sell for us. This same friend taught my mother how to write Haiku poetry. Writing poetry eventually became an excellent hobby for my mother providing a venue for expressing her emotions.

My brother David also remembers trips to Beacon Hill Park and going downtown with my mother while my father was away on the cable ship. She quietly put money aside for such occasions. He also remembers helping our mother water the vegetable garden and walking to the local dairy farm to buy a five-cent quart of milk. On the days my father had off from working on the cable ship, he would arrive home carrying boxes of Japanese oranges, coconuts, and other treats and was greeted with squeals of delight from all of us little children.

My brother David fondly recalls playing with his friends Raymond and David Hanson and watching their father build things. The boys had fun building their own soap-box cart from an apple box using rope for steering. These boys all attended Cedar Hill Elementary School a mile and a half from their homes. On the walk, they enjoyed eating the juicy apples which they plucked off the trees along the roadside. During recess they had fun sliding down a solid rock hill on their backsides. I remember watching them go off to school, books in hand, passing the large oak trees while shadows of the oak leaves danced off their backs as they ate their apples. Later, when the U.S. and Canada became involved in the war with Japan and the Canadian government forced the Japanese Canadians to leave the West Coast, the Hanson's brought us hand- knitted toques, mitts, and socks when they came to say goodbye.

After the fish cannery season ended my mother's youngest sister — my Auntie Lily, fondly known as "Tomichan" often came to babysit. David remembers how he and the others often snuggled up to her while she knitted. When my Auntie Lily's fiancé Ming Mah came over to visit sometimes brother David would be allowed to climb into Ming's green Ford Coupe. He then would attempt to work the long floor gear shift. What a lot of fun for a young boy.

Oak trees also graced our property. There was a large hollow made by the enormous roots where we children played house. Much to our delight the chickens laid their eggs in there as well, making it a treat for us to go looking for the eggs.

1940-Courtesy Family Collection - Victoria, Diane (standing)-
David (far left) clockwise- Amy, Sumi, George (Ken, away).

My sister Amy and I often visited my grandmother, Auntie Lily and my Uncle Soichi and Aunt Kimi Nakata. I have memories of being carried onto their fishing boat in Ucluelet in the Nootka Sound on the western side of Vancouver Island.

Although my parents continued to eke out a living and our material possessions were still meager, life in Victoria was a great improvement compared to the harsh days living in the Kelowna shed. They now owned their own home, and because the Depression had lifted by the end of the thirties, the economy was improving. Life in Victoria was relatively calm for my parents, and by 1942 three more children were added to their growing family: my sister Amy was born in 1936; I was born in 1938, and my brother George in 1939.

1941- Courtesy Family Collection - Victoria, Sumi,
Amy beside George on David's knee

Pearl Harbor

Suddenly our lives changed with catastrophic news-Pearl Harbor, Hawaii had been bombed by Japan. The Hanson boys were the first to deliver the news to us. It was December 7, 1941, and my Auntie Lily was down from Ucluelet following the cannery season. She babysat us while my mother did housework for others. We heard rumors everywhere that Japanese Americans were being evicted from their own homes. We couldn't help but worry that the same thing might happen in Canada.

Japanese Canadians lived all along the coast of British Columbia; many lived on the Gulf islands with acres and acres of property.

Rose Murakami of Salt Spring writes in her story "Ganbaru"- '*In 1941, there were 77 adults and children in 11 families. They owned in total about 1040 acres of land and ran some of the island's largest and most prosperous farms and businesses.*' [5]

My late husband Matsu's uncle, Gontaro Kadonaga owned 160 acres of land on Mayne Island and started a successful poultry

---

5 Ganbaru: the Murakami Family of Salt Spring Island by Rose Murakami, Japanese Garden Society of Salt Spring Island, 1992

business.[6] Gontaro Kadonaga and other pioneers were instrumental in developing Mayne Island.

While the main population of Japanese Canadians lived in Steveston BC and around Vancouver BC, others lived throughout the province in places like Ocean Falls, Woodfibre, the Gulf Islands, Pitt Meadows, Haney, Ruskin, Prince Rupert, etc., working hard to make a living and endeavoring to be good Canadian citizens.

As previously mentioned, my maternal Uncle Soichi and Aunt Kimi Nakata and Grandmother Nakata and my Auntie Lily, lived in Nootka Sound in Ucuelet. Another maternal Aunt Kimiye and Uncle Shuzo Tsubota lived in Port Alberni. My father and Uncle Shuzo were working in Britannia Beach when news reached them of the bombing of Pearl Harbor. One can only imagine the commotion, the uncertainty and anxiety caused by rumors of what was happening to the Japanese Americans in the United States. It was inevitable that the Japanese Canadians in Canada would be affected as well.

Dr. Henry Shimizu describes the backdrop of the political situation during this time:

> Whether for security or economic reasons, many of the B.C. politicians and the media demanded the removal of all Japanese Canadian communities along the West Coast of British Columbia. It seemed that the British Columbia government and the Federal government wished to isolate and eradicate the Japanese presence in the province, a form of "ethnic cleansing" from this part of Canada. The Federal Government used the

---

6 Tracing Our History to Tottori Ken Japan -2010 Ontario Tottori Ken Jin Kai Book Committee: Mary Mori, Brampton Ontario. Publisher, 4 Print, Mississauga, Ontario.

War Measures Act and Orders in Council as the
instruments to set their intentions into motion.
No similar action had ever been used against any
other Canadians or ethnic group in Canada.[7]

At the beginning of 1942, the United States government removed
all Japanese Americans from the west coast of mainland USA
(excluding Hawaii) and placed them in military type internment
camps. Soon after the Canadian Government followed suit and
ordered all people of Japanese ancestry to be removed from the
"protected area along the BC coast."

During the spring and summer of 1942, 22,000 people of Japanese
ancestry, over one-half of whom had been born in Canada, were
moved out of the West Coast. Although many families moved
east of the Rockies, about half of the deportees were settled into
internment camps in the interior of BC.

The bombing of Pearl Harbor by Japan started a chain of events
which would forever change lives not only worldwide but specifi-
cally in the Japanese community. Our lifestyle was soon to experience a major upheaval.

---

7 Shimizu, Dr. Henry- Images of Internment- (Victoria, BC: Tri- Press, 2008),1X

Evacuation

One day the rumors of the Japanese Canadians being evacuated became a reality. I vaguely remember my mother reading a letter. There was so much urgency and anxiety in her voice followed by a lot of people whispering and hustling and bustling about. That letter must have been the notice to evacuate. It was early 1942, about twelve weeks after the start of the war with Japan. All people of Japanese ancestry had suddenly become "enemy aliens" and were to be removed from the West Coast beyond the 100 mile protected zone. "Military necessity" was the justification for this mass removal and incarceration, despite the fact that senior members of Canada's military and the RCMP had opposed the action arguing that Japanese Canadians posed no threat to security. Major Ken Stuart had said "from the army point of view the Japanese does (sic) not constitute the slightest threat to national security."[8]

My Auntie Lily, who was still with us, said that Japanese books, cameras, and radios had to be destroyed. She never did return to Ucluelet to say good-bye to Uncle Ming with whom she was engaged to be married. The ring he gave her hung around her neck. When would she see him again?

----

8 Japanese Canadian Journey: The Nakagama Story-N. Rochelle Yamagishi; Trafford Publishing, Victoria, BC., 2010.

My sister Amy remembers the tar paper we had to put on the windows during blackout nights before the evacuation. It was frightening for us children not knowing what was going on. We had been warned that we had light showing from the windows and we better correct it before we were fined. These blackout practices on the West Coast were deemed mandatory to thwart any Japanese bombers who might fly over British Columbia. There was also a dusk to dawn curfew imposed on the Japanese and anyone caught breaking the curfew was liable to severe consequences including confinement in a prisoner of war camp in Angler, Ontario. It was in such a camp that my mother's brother Uncle Willie was held in Petawawa, Ontario for breaking curfew. We were certainly treated like enemy aliens. The men working out of town hurriedly rushed home.

My siblings and I were totally unaware of the anti-Japanese sentiments surfacing all around us. There are stories of students being abused by their teachers and fellow students, racist remarks spoken loudly in the adults' presence, along with rumors of submarines being present in the waters along the BC coast. A Japanese Canadian student recalls being called a "Jap," which meant she must be bad.

Japanese Canadians living on the west coast of Vancouver Island had only 48 hours to evacuate. My family in Victoria had slightly more time to pack but was allowed only two suitcases each. My Auntie Lily helped us pack what little we were able to take. My sister Amy and I had red and silver wagons, and we cried and cried when informed that we couldn't take the wagons with us. I remember being told that soldiers would watch over the wagons and our house. My brother Ken remembers our friends the Hanson's measuring all our feet so that when we returned they would know how much we had grown. It was on this occasion that they gave us the socks, toques, and gloves for our evacuation trip. The excitement felt by my siblings thinking we were going on a trip was in stark contrast to the confusing emotions of anger, sadness and fear of the unknown felt by our parents. There was a feeling of helplessness and defeat as there was no choice but to obey the authorities.

Assets including land, homes including contents which were left, businesses, boats and cars were seized and placed under the protection of the Custodian of Enemy Alien Properties. Other properties owned by our community, like language schools, temples, churches, and even hospitals were seized. My Uncle Soichi's fishing boat in Ucuelet was one of 1200 boats rounded up and seized.

#3190-Courtesy VPL- Confiscated boats rounded up.

My mother's poignant poem said it all:

My Mother's Senryu

Sumi narete tochi owarete sokai suru.
(Expelled, chased out from the land we lived comfortably)
Rokunin no ashi kata nokoshi sokai suru
(Evacuation, six small kid's foot prints left behind.)
Sutsu kaisu sageta kodomo wa ureshi garu
(Carrying suitcases, kids were so excited)
Shin pai wa doko e yukuno ka kane mo nai shi.
(No money, destination not known, so worried.)
Jinsei no ayumi tsuka reta, shiroi hata
(Tired, exhausted of this journey, defeated with white flag)

English translation by Taeko Morisawa.

The Cattle Stalls

Hastings Park

The rounding up of the Japanese Canadians had already begun in various parts of the province before we were moved out. We were literally being chased out, sent away to unknown, unfamiliar places as described in my mother's poem. In March 1942, we boarded the Canadian Pacific ship, Princess Patricia, in Victoria; my siblings and I with our suitcases were enthusiastic about going on a trip. When we arrived in Vancouver, my brothers half-carried, half- dragged the two large duffle bags allowed per family off of the ship and along the street before arriving at our new home: **Hastings Park, Vancouver BC.** How shocked we were to find that these stinky animal stalls were to become our home; wooden bunk beds with straw- filled mattresses and horse blankets became our sleeping accommodations. Blankets and sheets of all sizes and colors were used to cover the stalls for privacy.

Courtesy Nikkei National Museum (NNM)- Hastings
Park- Women' Dorm-1994-69-3-20

Courtesy NNM-Hastings Park- Baggage Room-1994-69-3-26

#1346- Courtesy Vancouver Public Library (VPL)-
Soldiers filling mattresses with straw.

All in all, over 22,000 Japanese were forcibly removed from the restricted area, a 100-mile strip up the Pacific West Coast, by the War Measures Act. We became one family of hundreds who were herded like cattle into the smelly animal stalls of Hastings Park (now known as the Pacific National Exhibition). Some described the nauseous smell as a combination of dried manure and tobacco smoke. We were told we would be there temporarily while the authorities decided what to do with us, when in fact our stay was prolonged by six months.

Many men were separated from their families and sent to road camps on the Hope-Princeton highway in southern BC or the Kootenays.[9] Others were sent to the interior of British Columbia to build housing for the incarceration of the evacuees. It was very

9 Righting Canada's wrongs: Japanese Canadian Internment in the Second World War: Pamela Hickman and Masako Fukawa; Japanese Canadian Journey: The Nakagama Story: N. Rochelle Yamagishi

difficult for the men to leave their wives and families behind not knowing what was to become of them. Communicating with each other was painful and slow in some of the remote areas where they worked, and their mail was always censored.

#1384- Courtesy VPL-Men saying good-bye- off to road camps.

Some families who were able to support themselves managed to move independently to other parts of British Columbia. They were able to do this without government interference and chose places to live in Eastern Canada or other small towns in BC outside the 100-mile protected zone. They were also able to stay together as families and were called "self-supporting families." Another way some families learned they could stay together was by going to Alberta or Manitoba as laborers on the sugar beet farms where there were worker shortages. Sadly, despite the fact that these families were able to stay together, they were met with much hostility, hard labor and unpleasant living conditions.

Fortunately, because our family was so large, my father was exempt from going to the road camps and we were able to remain together at Hastings Park. However, my father had to live in separate quarters with other men and older boys.

My brother Ken remembers hearing, "Shikataganai" (it can't be helped) over and over again from the people at Hastings Park and later in New Denver. It was the sad and compelling refrain of our people which described the hopelessness and resignation the Japanese Canadians felt during this period in our lives. They believed that one's fate is beyond one's control.

However, the "shikataganai" philosophy also gave them the impetus to go on, to cooperate with the government and "ganbaru" (to persevere). Making the best of their circumstances by submitting to the government policies, it helped to prove their loyalty as Canadian citizens.

Each of the animal stalls (our bedrooms) held two bunk beds. I had a top bunk and could look over the whole building from my bed. So much for privacy! Recently I saw a picture of what we called, "horse blankets." They were, in fact, army blankets that were issued to each family. They were grey, wool edged with black stitching. I remember my family using them for years after the war. My cousin Sandi (Mah) Sasaki remembers seeing them at her mother's (Auntie Lily's) house for years as well.

Courtesy NNM Hastings Park-Blanket Distribution Room-1994-69-7

Fortunately day passes were available from the RCMP for people to go downtown or visit friends who were still around in the city. Therefore, my Auntie Lily was able to see her fiancé Ming Mah several times during her stay in Hastings Park.

When the annual Pacific National Exhibition took place during that summer, a barbed wire enclosure surrounded the Agricultural buildings. Instead of the cows, horses, pigs, etc. being exhibited, summer of 1942 saw over a thousand black haired, Canadian Japanese men, women, and children occupying the buildings and the animal stalls.

Children were able to adapt to their surroundings quite readily. My brother David found the sudden availability of new friends a great way to keep busy.

When the children weren't attending the makeshift school in the sports auditorium, they climbed fences, practiced judo (which a neighbor's father had taught them), and made slingshots from the rubber bands they removed from the insides of golf balls.

Courtesy NNM Hastings Park- Building L- Classroom-1994-69-3-23

They then made paper ammos into marbles and shot at each other from the top bunks. My siblings and I were spared much anguish, but our parents went through some heart wrenching times facing an uncertain future. The park had become the assembly centre for the Japanese Canadians being sent from outside of Vancouver. There was a chain-linked fence around the park and a huge German shepherd dog guarded the entrance reminding all of the incarceration.

Northwest Nikkei News reporter Ed Suguro wrote about the crowded, unhealthy conditions at Hastings Park in his February 1990 article which my late sister explained to him. Minor epidemics of measles, mumps, and food poisoning spread quickly through our community. People constantly had to be put in isolation. My cousin Reiko had scarlet fever and my brothers David and Ken had mumps. They were quarantined in the makeshift hospital.

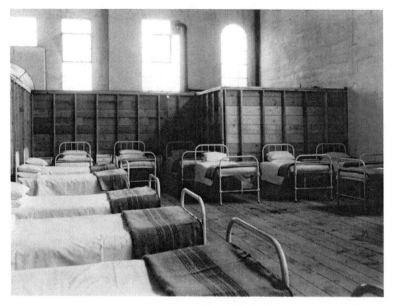

Courtesy NNM- makeshift hospital room.

Mary Ohara, a former internee and resident of Hastings Park recalled coming down with mumps and being isolated in the so-called hospital where there was no space available for her.[10] She was relegated to the "dungeon," an underground storage space for coal and animal feed which was cleared out to make room for the sick. She said it was one of the scariest events of her life — a nightmare to have to get up and go to the bathroom in the middle of the night and to hear children screaming for their parents at all hours of the night.

Being among the first arrivals at Hastings Park, she and her family couldn't get over the putrid smell of the dried animal manure still being scraped off the concrete floors while soldiers madly scram-bled to fill mattresses with straw for the crude wooden bunk beds. It was not long before the straw got damp, moldy and infested by

10 Righting Canada's Wrongs: Japanese Canadian Internment in the Second World War, Pamela Hickman and Masako Fukawa, James Lorimer &Co. Ltd., Publishers, Toronto.

bedbugs. She was covered with red welts from the bites. The soldiers eventually sprayed all the beds with DDT.

Initially, people had to use metal animal watering troughs as toilets until proper facilities were installed. Small children needed to put their little feet on apple crates in order to balance themselves and not fall into the trough. Later, a plank of wood with holes in it was placed over the metal troughs, and eventually makeshift partitions were placed around each hole to provide a semblance of privacy. Water ran through the troughs. It was here in the latrine my brother Ken lost his hand-knitted green sweater in the toilet. My Auntie Lily recalled many women coming down with diarrhea from the strange foods they ate, and she saw several of these ladies faint as they exited the toilets.

I remember sitting with my brother George in the children's cafeteria where my Auntie Lily worked in the children's kitchen and where her brother, my Uncle Soichi, worked as a cook's helper. We looked forward to my Auntie serving us. It was comforting to see her presence. My sister Amy remembers the tin plate and tin cup they had to take each time to the mess hall, "where they dumped yucky carrots, potato, and meat onto the plate."

Courtesy NNM-Hastings Park- Children's Cafeteria-1994-69-3-16

Courtesy NNM-Hastings Park-Adult Dining Room-1994-69-3-142

1942- Courtesy Family Collection- Hastings Park
Front Row-Adults sitting- Naoye Morisawa, Grandma Nakata, Aunt Kimiye Nakata, Aunt Kimi Tsubota.
Back Row- Adults standing-Auntie Lily, Diane, Uncle Soichi Nakata.
(Missing — Kanekichi Morisawa, Uncle Shuzo Nakata).

It really was an excruciatingly painful time for many. So many women with husbands away working at road camps or away building houses for the internees had to fend for themselves and their children with very little communication from their husbands as to their whereabouts and welfare. These women and their families were sent like we were to small town relocation camps in the B.C. interior — places like New Denver, Slocan, Sandon, and Lemon Creek, Bay Farm, etc. Later the men were finally allowed to reunite with their families. Those who resisted the moves or challenged the orders of the Canadian government were rounded up and imprisoned.

Six months after our initial admission to Hastings Park, early fall saw us being loaded onto a train headed for New Denver, BC our new destination.

"The Orchard", New Denver

114 Marine Drive

THIS WAS THE TOWN FIRST KNOWN AS ELDORADO; LATER IT BECAME NEW DENVER WHEN IT WAS FORECAST IT WOULD BECOME GREATER THAN ITS NAMESAKE, DENVER, COLORADO. BY 1893 NEW DENVER WAS ESTABLISHED AS THE WESTERN GATEWAY TO THE SILVER COUNTRY. CLOSE BY, SILVER-LEAD PROPERTIES LIKE THE MOUNTAIN CHIEF, ALPHA, CALIFORNIA, ALAMO AND OTHERS CONTRIBUTED TO THE GENERAL PROSPERITY OF THE TOWN. TO THE EAST, SANDON, WHITEWATER, THREE FORKS, CODY AND OTHER MINING TOWNS BECKONED. TODAY THE ORIGINAL BANK OF MONTREAL AND A DOZEN OTHER BUILDINGS FROM THE TURN OF THE CENTURY STAND AS MUTE REMINDERS OF THE DAYS WHEN THIS TOWN WAS CONSIDERED THE NEW ELDORADO.

Courtesy Private Collection- Sign outside New Denver

New Denver, isolated but nestled between the Arrow and Kootenay Lakes, was situated on Slocan Lake. It was a former ghost town that went from boom to bust but once had high hopes of becoming a large city like Denver, Colorado. New Denver became our next home. It was an idyllic little town lying deep in the Kootenay Valley. It was one of five internment centers and the largest camp situated on the lake. With the Kokanee Glacier looking imposingly down on the lake, it made a pretty picture in contrast to the gloomy fate of the "enemy aliens".

Courtesy Private Collection- Slocan Lake
Beach- New Denver- Our favorite site

Being among the crowd of approximately 1,550 internees heading into New Denver, we were hustled into a CPR Rail train, and the smoke and black soot from the steam engine filled the coach. My brother David had an infected burn on his left elbow and he remembers how the putrid smoke and soot in the air prolonged the healing.

New Denver was once a mining and logging area, and when the Japanese Canadians arrived, only a few white families lived there. Some of the town's children were armed with rocks and sticks to greet the evacuees. Having never seen Japanese people before, they were scared and curious. Fortunately, there were no incidents. My late sister Diane's memories of arriving in New Denver are revealed in her interview with reporter Ed Suguro of the Northwest Nikkei News.

She recalled how the arrival of the Japanese created a boom in New Denver. The few businesses they had — the grocery store, general mercantile store and the service station — were suddenly blessed with new customers.

On what was once a regular orchard, space was created for housing the internees in very small shacks. That was how the area where we were interned received the nickname "The Orchard."

Courtesy NNM- Model of New Denver- "The Orchard"

While my family was waiting for one of the 275 shacks to be ready, we first had to live in large tents. On one occasion my brother George got a nasty burn on his chin from a hot stick while we were cooking on an open fire outside. That burn, like my brother David's, took a while to heal.

My brothers hiked around a lot to get familiarized with their new surroundings. They once climbed a steep hill that was completely cleared. It turned out to be a skid road for logs that came hurtling down the hill while they were still climbing. They quickly jumped aside and managed to survive unhurt.

With winter just around the corner, we finally moved into the hastily built, tar papered shacks made of rough, green lumber. Spaces could be seen between the boards. A few families still lived in tents at the onset of winter. We were one of the luckier families, as those who remained in the tents were surrounded by deep snow.

That first winter of 1942 was reportedly one of the harshest in the Slocan Valley. In the morning, my brother David remembers seeing frost- covered nail heads looking like buttons on the walls. Other people remember scraping buckets of frost off the walls. I recall later that year my father and my uncles trying to insulate the walls using large pieces of cardboard. I remember having achy knees during those cold winters and my father applying warm compresses on them to alleviate the pain.

Because we were a large family of eight, we occupied an entire large shack which was 14 feet by 28 feet, a total of 392 square feet. It had two small bedrooms on either side of a common room which included a stove and cooking area. I remember sleeping in one room with my mother, father and brother George, until my youngest brother Allan Isao was born in March, 1944. Then I moved in with the other four siblings in the second little bedroom which had two bunk beds. I slept with my oldest sister Diane on the narrow, lower bunk. Three or four layers of horse blankets saw us through that first harsh winter.

Courtesy Private Collection- Typical Shack- New Denver

My brother Allan was born with a thymus gland disorder. My sister Amy remembers how my mother had to get special permission from the RCMP for regular trips to Nelson for Allan's radiation treatments.

Courtesy Family Collection- Allan and
Amy- N.D.- Rockery Garden-1945

Smaller families had to share a shack with a second family and take turns cooking and cleaning. For many families, it was a stressful and uncomfortable time having to share such small quarters with strangers.

Cook stoves helped heat the shacks while coal oil lamps and candles provided light. Our shacks were also furnished with a table, benches and some shelving made by Japanese Canadian carpenters.

Courtesy Private Collection-New Denver- Inside View of Shack

These same creative carpenters built a Japanese-style bathhouse with room for men on one side, women on the other. On each side was a large wooden tub filled with water heated by a firebox under the tubs, and basins and little stools for sitting. There was a place for shoes on entering and a raised area for changing. Standard protocol involved scooping up water with a basin to rinse off, then another basin of water was used to wash and rinse off again. Only then was one allowed to go into the tub to sit and soak for a while much like a modern day hot tub. It was a relaxing, soothing experience for most of us, but my best memory was of swimming in the tub with other little girls. For the adults, it was a place to socialize, gossip or hear the latest news about the war. I once woke up crying, completely disoriented at the bathhouse. Apparently, I walked all the way from our house, through the backyard garden, and to the bathhouse in my sleep. My mother came and fetched me saying that the last time she saw me I was sound asleep on our bed at home.

Our bathrooms were outhouses with three stalls on each side, one side for women, the other for men. These outhouses were shared by several families. Sometimes it was so cold in the winter it was hard to pee. Eventually my mother kept a small can under the bed for us to use during the cold months. But for the other mode of relief, we still needed to trudge through the snow to the outhouses. Not much fun, that's for sure.

Courtesy Private Collection- Outhouse- 3
stalls- Nikkei Memorial Centre

That first winter I entered kindergarten while the others went to school. Each class was taught by teachers who had only been trained the previous summer. The next year I clearly remember my first day of school going into grade one. Excitedly lined up with all the big kids in front of the row of shacks which served as our classrooms, I strained to hear my name being called. I waited and waited to be called until everyone had gone into their classrooms, and I was the only one left standing. A kind teacher finally led me to my classroom but not before I burst into tears. What an embarrassment on my first day of school, it certainly tempered my excitement of finally getting into grade one. Fortunately it never spoiled my love for school.

Courtesy Private Collection- Sumi's New Denver Kindergarten Class
Graduation Class-1946
Sumi- see arrow 2nd row, Cousin Reiko-front row 2nd from right
Friend Amy Nagata-back row center

Courtesy Private Collection- Sumi's gr. 3 girl classmates- New Denver
Left to row- Lucy Hoshino, Sumi Morisawa, Harriet Iwase,
Machiko Uchida, Chieko Oka, Jane Tanaka

We lived on a street where water taps were located at several inter-
vals along the street. Water was carried in buckets from here into
the homes, but usually women used the taps to wash their rice. In
the wintertime some young people poured water on the street in
front of our house to make the road a sheet of ice, and we went
sleigh riding. Fortunately, no one had cars to drive on that slip-
pery street.

The mercantile store ordered Japanese food for the evacuees, so
the people were fairly well supplied. My sister Amy remembers
my mother tearing the coupons which allotted each family their
quota of eggs, butter, and sugar. The butter was actually a white
margarine which we mixed with a yellow powder to simulate the
real thing.

Most of the families, including our own, had a backyard vegetable garden to provide additional food. My father and my older brothers and sisters carried water from the lake to water our garden. Most plants like potatoes, kabocha pumpkins, and other leafy vegetables grew well in the virgin soil. Adding to the garden vegetables and the food purchased with our coupons, we picked fiddleheads and dandelion leaves from the hillside. These wild plants had to be soaked in water to remove their bitter taste, but when cooked and eaten with a little soya sauce, they made an appetizing vegetable dish.

Some of our people built rowboats and fished in the lake, or in the fall they would row to the other side of the lake to pick matsutake (pine mushrooms — a valuable commodity today).

One day my father rowed my brother George and me across the lake to Silverton to pick cherries. That winter we ate so many canned cherries I got sick of them. To this day, canned cherries remind me of New Denver.

We also bought cherries and apples from Thring's Ranch while Campbell's Dairy delivered milk to the New Denver homes. So with the fruit, homegrown vegetables, wild mushrooms and wild plants our diet was well supplemented.

Our front yard sloped down from the road to our house. Here my father built a beautiful rock garden similar to that of our neighbors, the Onoderas. These two gardens were featured on a postcard.

Courtesy Family Collection- Amy, George, Sumi, David, Ken,
Diane, Dad, Allan- beside rockery garden New Denver

As life in New Denver was quite laid back, people still needed to find ways to make money and occupy themselves.

My father, using the skills he learned on the cable ship while living in Victoria, worked as an assistant cook in the sanatorium which housed many residents with tuberculosis. My grandmother eventually became one of those patients suffering TB. After the war was over this same sanatorium was used as a school and housed the Sons of Freedom Doukhobor children.

Courtesy NNM-Sanitarium- New Denver-1992-33-22

There was always a need for services in our community. Some maintained the bathhouse; others delivered the mail and groceries; some worked in the post office. Many young men went logging while others worked in the sawmill. Some of the women either taught Japanese language classes or gave sewing lessons. One woman opened her own beauty parlor. My Auntie Lily took sewing lessons. Using her own pattern, she made a beautiful wedding dress for her friend. She made matching polka dot dresses for my sister Amy and me. Being an excellent knitter, Auntie also knitted wool, two-piece dresses for us. We benefitted from her sewing, knitting, and crocheting skills for many ensuing years.

I have memories of long, lazy summer days at the beach on Slocan Lake with my siblings. I swam (dog-paddled) out on the lake until the water got dark green at a big drop off, and then I paddled back to shore. It's a wonder I never drowned.

The camp had a community hall which held dances and concerts and showed Japanese movies. The main sporting event in town was baseball, where the young men could expend some energy. Arts and crafts flourished in the camp as well as did many cultural events. Everyone had a way of keeping busy but being a small community they also knew everybody's business.

My two oldest brothers David and Ken hiked along Carpenter Creek to Three Forks and picked mouthwatering huckleberries in the long summer months. When they weren't picking berries they fished for suckers and squaw fish at the mouth of the same Carpenter Creek where a gold rush once took place. They once found gold flakes which unfortunately turned out to be iron pyrite (fool's gold). They were also fortunate to be able to join the Boy Scouts which was led by a Lutheran minister. My brother David passed his Tenderpak level.

Another evacuation relocation center was a place called Roseberry which was at the end of the Canadian Pacific Rail line from the

Okanagan. It was to this place that my two uncles and aunts moved with their families before leaving for Japan and where my two oldest brothers walked to visit these relatives. David and Ken often got sick during these two-mile walks — either from sunstroke or from drinking the water from the hillside along the way — or both.

My younger brother George was hospitalized for a short time to have a cyst removed on his neck. He cried and cried when my parents had to leave after visiting hours, but some of the patients taking pity on him, gave him some pennies to play with. When asked what he was going to do with the pennies, George replied, "I'm going to buy my dad some tobacco." Another time George had a tooth removed under anesthesia, and my mother piggy-backed him home. My brother George also remembers looking deeply into a water puddle one day, becoming frightened and crying at the reflection of the sky he saw there.

For the most part, life was carefree for all the children. I can't imagine what it was like for the grownups, but they did what they could with what life gave them and they made the best of it. My mother admitted that in spite of the stressful situation, the years she spent in New Denver and Slocan were the first ones spent free of hard physical labor since her marriage began. It was a strange way to have a holiday. The RCMP's periodic tours of our relocation center were a stark reminder that our four years here were hardly a holiday. Barbed wire fences and watchtowers were unnecessary as there was no place to escape. People had day- passes to go to nearby Nelson, but there were no reports of escapees. Before long, the air of uncertainty and insecurity which hung over us intensified, as rumors of the war ending filtered through the community in early 1945.

1945

The War Is Over

Soon there was talk of people moving here and there and of possible repatriation to Japan. By early 1945, the end of the war with Japan seemed close as the war in Europe was officially declared over. Some BC politicians began campaigning for the "voluntary" deportation of all people of Japanese origin regardless of citizenship. In the spring of 1945, notice was given to all the internees that everyone over sixteen years of age had to "voluntarily" choose between relocating east of the Rockies or repatriation to Japan. Many were born in Canada and hardly spoke any Japanese, but there were no options — "**either relocate east or go to Japan.**" The war with Japan concluded with the American bombing of Nagasaki and Hiroshima and Emperor Hirohito's surrender. The dispersion of the Japanese Canadians across Canada began, and those heading for Japan were collected in other internment camps like Roseberry.

My friend Amy Nagata and her family were an example of one of those families who moved out east to New Toronto, Ontario, while other families moved to further points east. Not having to enter Hastings Park, her family was moved from Ruskin, BC to Tashme (another internment center), and then to New Denver.

She, like many of us younger ones, did not feel the hardships felt by our parents. For her, New Denver was also an idyllic summer place with mountains, lake and forests all around. She and her family lived up the road from us on Marine Drive and remember the black bears foraging for garbage at the bridge crossing Carpenters Creek.

At first life was not easy for Amy and her family as they moved to Ontario. She and her family settled in a Summerville Hostel when they first moved to Etobicoke in the Greater Toronto area. A man called Mr. Tregunno from St. Catherines came by and offered them work picking peaches at his farm. So off they went. They lived in a Quonset hut (or Kamaboko house), and by the time peach season was over, it was very cold in the house. Because Mr. Tregunno also owned a basket factory in Mount Forest where many families were employed, they moved again to a subdivided former senator's house with other families and were able to work in the basket factory.

My friend Amy and her family were among 11,000 Japanese Canadians who were living in Ontario and scattered all over the province. When restrictions for entering the professions were finally lifted, eventually the Japanese Canadians living out east were able to get jobs in every line of work including the professions such as engineering, medicine, law, teaching, nursing and architecture, etc. My friend Amy became a schoolteacher.

Other families went to Alberta or farther east to Manitoba where they took whatever work they could find. Still others, completely disillusioned with Canada like our relatives, and feeling bruised, battered and betrayed took the option of returning to Japan.

With the loss of their livelihood, my maternal Uncle Soichi Nakata and his family, and my maternal Aunt Kimiye Tsubota and her family with Grandma Nakata were ready to leave Canada. They were one of many families who were moved to Roseberry while waiting to go abroad to Japan. Those who chose to go to Japan faced a war torn country on their arrival. With the country and the economy in shambles and the people living in desperate poverty, the citizens met the repatriates with much hostility. They said to the repatriates, "Why did you come to Japan? We don't want you; go back to Canada." Having had tuberculosis and diabetes along with the stress of travelling, Grandma Nakata's health rapidly deteriorated and she passed away shortly after her month -long boat trip and arrival in Japan.

My Auntie Lily was finally able to get married to Ming Mah at the courthouse in Nelson, BC on May 21st, 1944. While waiting to get her permit to return to the coast of BC, my Auntie Lily and her husband Ming lived in a one bedroom apartment in Calgary, Ab. In September 1945, they (because my uncle was Chinese) were allowed to return to the coast of BC.

American evacuees were freed from incarceration immediately after the war ended in 1945. Their homes were not confiscated or sold off without permission. We, in Canada, on the other hand, no longer owned our homes. Still banned from returning to the west coast, my parents were left to fend for themselves and the family. We had absolutely no assistance from the government to help resettle.

When the war was over we had to leave New Denver. Only those in dire straits were allowed to remain. By choosing not to go east of the Rockies or go "back" to Japan, we were forced to live in surrounding small towns wherever my father found work in order to support his family. My father found work in a logging camp and moved our family to nearby Slocan City, BC our next temporary home.

The "Ratty Place"

Slocan, BC

We lived in what one brother called "a Ratty Place" in Slocan, which was a very small 3 room place that was part of a larger building. Slocan was another former ghost town turned internment center. The Morishita family, also evacuees, lived next door and was extremely kind to us. Even though most radios were confiscated before the evacuation, the Morishitas had one in their living room. What a treat it was when they often invited us over to listen to their radio — especially to one of my favorite programs, "Baby Snooks." We also listened to the Hit Parade. Some of the top ten songs we remember from that time included "Smoke Gets in your Eyes" and "I'm Looking over a Four Leaf Clover". We sat motionless by the radio whenever "Inner Sanctum" or "The Green Hornet" came on. We read the entire Superman and Buck Rogers's comic books.

My brother David and his friend, Hajime Kinoshita (no relation to my late husband, Matsu Kinoshita.) found summer work peeling railway ties at the local sawmill for five cents a tie. This was an enormously difficult and heavy work for a couple of grade seven boys. My brothers David and Ken also worked hard chopping and cutting up the firewood we needed for our kitchen stove.

Although times were tough we still had a lot of fun, especially in the summer time when we played around the neighborhood nonchalantly unaware of the gravity of our situation. We had so little money and nowhere to permanently settle. My brothers fished off the old wooden bridge for Dolly Varden trout in the Slocan River. The water was so crystal clear you could see the fish swimming in the river. My brother Ken remembers catching a rainbow trout that was sixteen or seventeen inches long and felt like it weighed at least seven pounds. Several times they borrowed a row boat from friends and got swept along with the current and into the path of the log boom floating down the river. How they survived I'll never know.

We played with other Japanese Canadian children whose families were waiting to be transferred to permanent locations. The Caucasian neighbors living across the lane resented, bullied and teased us. On one occasion my brother David beat up the bully next door who was taunting and picking on my other brother Ken. My youngest brother George stuck his tongue out at a big tall guy who constantly teased him. When the bully pulled out a knife and said, "I'm going to cut your tongue off," George ran away.

We lived in Slocan for about a year and a half until my father got a job as head cook up at the Enterprise Mine in Silverton, BC making it necessary for us to move to the small mining town. By this time, the BC Security Commission no longer had any control over us, and we were finally able to regain our independence and freedom to live wherever we wanted. Ironically, we were still not free to return into the 100- mile protected zone. The town of Silverton became our next home.

The "Old Library"

Silverton, BC

Courtesy Private Collection-Silverton

Silverton was a picturesque little mining town situated on Slocan Lake between New Denver and Slocan. By the time we moved to Silverton my brother David was in grade nine, my brother Ken in grade eight, my sister Amy in grade six, I was in grade four and my brother George was in grade three. My oldest sister Diane quit school in grade 10 to help my parents up at the Enterprise mine, where my father was chief cook. My youngest brother, three year old Allan, lived with them up at the mining camp.

Courtesy Private Collection- Allan and George
Morisawa- Silverton-1948- Close to Library home

With both parents and my sister Diane working at the mine full time, we children essentially lived on our own. We lived in the bottom floor of a two-story building which was a former library. The dusty, old, antique books were housed in glass-door cupboards along one wall of our makeshift bedroom. Two double beds lined up beneath these cupboards. We occupied the entire bottom floor which included this bedroom and another small one at the rear of the building beside the little kitchen. There was a small living room in the front of the building. The outhouse was in the back yard.

Outside stairs led to the upper floor hall where Whist card-players gathered once a week. For three to four hours we tolerated the sounds of scraping chairs and loud talk. On the other hand, the United Church, who held their services next door to us every Sunday, had to tolerate our noises. We enjoyed skipping indoors and hitting shuttlecocks with the old library books. Repeated thumping from our house would always bring a church member over to knock at our door requesting that we stop the noise. Finally, after several requests, they actually invited us unruly heathens to Sunday school. I only attended once as I was annoyed that the teacher kept calling me "Emo."

When my parents came to visit us, what a delight it was to be given ice cream bars and other treats, long anticipated and much savored. My father enjoyed joining the other miners at the local watering hole (pub).

There were many carefree days especially in the summer months — biking, fishing off the pier at the lake, rafting, and playing badminton which my sister Amy especially enjoyed. Badminton games were organized in the community hall next door.

Courtesy Family Collection- Memorial Hall
Silverton- Reunion trip- 2009

There were yearly celebrations which New Denver, Silverton, and Slocan organized jointly and took turns hosting — the May long weekend, July 1st, and Labor Day holidays with special celebrations and track meets in which all our family participated. I remember my sister Amy participating in several events like walking on the greasy pole, participating in a diving contest (Amy did a beautiful belly flop!) and track and field, where she feels she hurt her back broad jumping. What a lot of fun we had taking part in those events.

My brothers fished off the pier using pieces of dough for bait on hooks fashioned out of a straight pin with a tree branch for their fishing pole. Trophies of bottom fish and suckers lined up on the pier beside them. Another day while double biking out of town two or three miles, my brothers David and Ken walked into a hornet's nest after they stopped to pick huckleberries. They panicked and ran down a hill, all the while being chased by hornets. Ken jumped off a small cliff and landed on top of their bicycle, bending the spokes all out of shape on their front wheel. They managed to straighten it out and double biked back home again.

Another time my brothers built a raft out of logs they found on the beach and sailed all over the lake, even though their swimming skills were very limited. One day their raft, made with rusty old nails, fell apart. My brothers David and Ken yelled to my brother George, who couldn't swim at all, "Hold on to a log!" They all made it to shore hanging on to logs for dear life. The next time they were out on a raft David and Ken threw George into the water to teach him how to swim. "Just paddle like a dog," they called out to him. George learned to swim quickly after that. My sister Amy remembers learning how to swim the same way — being pushed off the raft by her brothers and realizing she needed to figure out how to dog-paddle to shore or drown. Fortunately, I learned to swim on my own in New Denver.

We attended a two room school. Mrs. Bell taught grades one to four, and Mrs. Lind taught grades five to eight. We had fun times playing outside at noon and recess.

In the wintertime, my brothers went bobsledding. Four or five kids would pile on top of one another on one sled as they slid down a snow covered hill. When they hit a sharp curve, the sudden turn would send all the kids sprawling over the hillside.

My sister Amy and I wore bright red, oversized snowsuits sent to us from our paternal aunt in Ontario; the boys got green ones. It was easy to spot us coming, but we did remain warm in the wintertime.

The winter of 1948 was the first time in twenty years Slocan Lake froze over. The boys tested the lake by throwing large boulders on the ice. When the ice didn't crack, it was safe — a signal for all the kids to go skating. My brothers even rode their bikes on the ice when the lake froze over. After moving to Surrey the following year, we heard news of a teenager named Snooky Gordon falling through the ice to his death.

My siblings and I have "warm fuzzies" when we remember Silverton. My friends and I amused ourselves all day — skipping, having make-believe adventures, and playing with dolls. We were especially fond of the Nelson family. We were of similar ages to their children; in particular, Frankie, Junie and Georgie who were in the same grades as Amy, George and me.

We often played softball on the Nelson's front yard in the long summer evenings till twilight. Gordie Nelson was the oldest son who drove a ten ton Studebaker army ore truck back and forth from the Enterprise Mine. He was everybody's idol. He was a familiar sight driving up and down the main drag past our library home and he was always kind and friendly when he saw us. Whenever important issues had to be discussed with my parents, or report cards and consent forms needed to be signed by them, it was Gordon who would act as our courier or take my brother David up to the mine to see my parents.

My brother George and Georgie Nelson or Junie Nelson and I were frequent passengers with Gordon as he drove to and from the mine. While we were there, my sister Diane loaded us up with cookies to take back home.

Halloween was so much fun trick-or-treating all over town with our pillowcases. It was easy to cover the whole town in one evening and to gather a huge haul of goodies. One night the young people rode an old chuck wagon down the middle of the one and only main drag right down to the pier. That was another fun activity.

My sister Amy and I with a group of kids recalled "chivalrying" Gordon and Betty Nelson after their wedding. It was a custom of banging tin cans outside the door until the newlyweds gave out money.

Unfortunately, life was not all fun and games, as there were many responsibilities which needed to be dealt with. My eleven-year-old sister Amy did the cooking, and I helped while the boys looked after getting firewood. I don't remember what we had for meals, but wieners were often on the grocery list. My brothers remember eating a lot of bread and jam. I did the dishes, got groceries, and babysat my youngest brother Allan when he was down from the mine. We are grateful for what my sister Amy did at such a young age with so much responsibility.

Getting the firewood was no easy task for my brothers, either. In the summertime, my brothers David and Ken cut down trees with a bow saw and slashed off the branches. Then, with the logs cut into four-foot lengths, they piled them into one-cord blocks (four feet long by eight feet wide by four feet high). They had four to five cords by September before school started. A friend named Sam helped truck the cords down to our house. My brother David recalls, "When Sam was hung over from a drunken night before, he would gear down to the lowest gear and have me take over driving down a curvy logging road. When we got to the highway, Sam would take over again." Our neighbor, Mr. Didrikson, would buzz-saw the logs into stove-sized lengths for us. We helped him, as it was a three person job. The saw was powered by a pulley on the back of a Model "A" Ford car. What would we have done for firewood had my brothers David and Ken not worked so hard getting the wood?

On occasion, my sister Amy went up to the mine on the weekend to help my parents. Her job was to wash and wipe all the dishes and hang out the laundered towels to dry before going to bed around 11 o'clock at night. She remembers seeing large black bears roaming around the camp trying to get at the meat hung in the cold storage. One time she remembers eating a whole pumpkin pie my father had baked. Amy was unhappy when she saw my father being so hard on my mother and my oldest sister Diane.

Other than helping out where we could, my younger brother George and I were spared a lot of responsibilities, thanks to my older siblings who bore much of the burden.

Diane, our oldest sister, 16-years-old and great with child, left Silverton early to live with my Auntie Lil and Uncle Ming, who by then were living in Vancouver. While in Vancouver, Diane entered business school. After the baby was born and adopted out and Diane graduated from school, she ultimately worked for the CT Takahashi and Co. in Vancouver where she met her future husband, Tom Iwata.

Even with our parents working up at the mine, we managed on our own. We had a roof over our heads, a warm place to sleep, food to eat, and clothes to wear. We had friends to play with and a school to attend. With the little we had, we managed to survive.

We heard that B.C. was still a hostile place and the "Japs" were still not allowed to return to the coast although the war was over and we were no longer a perceived threat. Those who tried to return were arrested and jailed.

The Ban Is Lifted

1949

The War Measures Act had been lifted as early as 1945 in Canada but we were still treated as enemy aliens. The Canadian government, unlike the Americans began their policy of dispersal across Canada or repatriating citizens to Japan. Also, by then the U.S. government had already begun allowing Japanese Americans back to the coast. It was not until the summer of 1949 when Canada lifted the ban that would allow the Japanese Canadians to return to the coast.

As I mentioned before, our home had been confiscated. An Order-in-Council (P.C. 1665) gave the BC Security Commission, which was established on March 4, 1942, the power to make bylaws, hold property and enter into contracts.[11] All properties (including our home and our little wagons) the evacuees were unable to take with them were confiscated and placed under the protective custody of "The Custodian of Enemy Properties." This meant the properties should have been returned after the war.

---

11 Japanese Canadian Journey: The Nakagama Story, N. Rochelle Yamagashi, Trafford Publishing, Victoria, BC, 2010.

This order in council was reversed in 1943 when the BC Security Commission passed another Order-in-Council declaring that all properties held in trust were to be **sold or auctioned off without permission of their owners.** This was another betrayal of trust. I later learned the proceeds from the sale of the properties and goods were used to pay for our incarceration as enemy aliens. This applied to all evacuees.

Therefore, there was no chance of ever returning to our home in Victoria. A meager amount of money was sent to our parents from the sale of our home, property and whatever was left behind. We didn't have a lot but it was still our home. It is difficult trying to describe what happened to thousands of people with sizable amounts of valuable property, possessions and businesses — all of which were taken away and sold for a pittance. Others had their belongings stolen by people who promised to look after them.

With the meager earnings my father, mother and sister saved from working in the Enterprise Mining Camp, and my brother David's small monetary contribution, my father decided for the sake of our education that it was time to move out of Silverton. My sister Diane dropped out of high school to help my parents cook up at the Enterprise Mine. That was her significant contribution to the family's earnings to purchase property.

David remembers my father taking several trips to the West Coast and getting in touch with a few Japanese farmers who had just moved into Surrey. Heeding their advice, my father, with the help of my Uncle Ming and Auntie Lily, spent hours scouting out potential farm land. They finally found fifteen acres of raw land. My father was able to put a down payment on the place in South Surrey close to White Rock, BC. At long last, our family moved back to the west coast of BC.

"The Farm"

15460 32nd Ave.

(formerly called Brown Rd.)

South Surrey, BC

I'll never forget the trip out to the coast on the Greyhound bus via the Hope Princeton Highway. Because parts of the highway were still under construction, the road was long and winding, and I spent most of the time retching with my head in a vomit bag. Then excitedly, we finally saw the glimpse of a city as we crossed over Pattullo Bridge into New Westminster.

It was 1949, and my father was 51 years old, my mother 41 years old. Our family of six children (because Diane was already in Vancouver) with meager possessions, began life anew. Although we faced some extreme challenges, we were once again property owners.

The fifteen-acre parcel was covered with enormous Douglas fir stumps. On the parcel was a small four bedroom house which was not a whole lot bigger than the shack we occupied in New Denver. There was a large two-story chicken house beside the woodshed close to an outhouse about fifty feet away from the house, and an old pigpen at the back of the property across the creek.

Like pioneers, my father and the boys cleared the land of huge old-growth Douglas fir tree stumps throughout the property that first winter. By this time my brothers, David and Ken, now teenagers, worked like grown men helping my father dynamite the huge stumps. My sister Amy, brother George and I picked up wood strewn all around by the blasting to feed the bonfires. This was the beginning of many years of real hard labor on the farm for all of us. By springtime the land in front of the chicken house was cleared of the large pile of tree stumps. My father ploughed the front section. I'll never forget all that couch grass. With large shovels hammered into giant hoes, the men loosened the grass. Inch by inch, the rest of us shook the tangled couch grass roots free from the dirt leaving pile upon pile of straw-looking roots. This was tedious, back breaking work.

Eventually, after the land was prepared, we grew vegetables which my father sold in town to help put food on the table. We also raised chickens for their eggs and got meat from the chickens and pigs. My sister Amy and I had to clean the chicken coop and the pigpen and even helped spread manure on the fields.

That first year, enough land was cleared on the rear property as well to plant our first crop of strawberries in the springtime. Eventually the back acreage soon became a beautiful strawberry patch of at least five acres or more. Every year we went through the routine of hoeing and weeding, fertilizing, cutting off runners, and replanting and replacing the old plants. Then we cut off the tops of the plants at season's end. We did this routine row after row, season after season. When the strawberries were ripe, pickers including some school friends came to pick the beautiful luscious strawberries. They provided a nice respite for us as well as being good company.

Courtesy family collection- strawberry pickers.

Courtesy family collection-old pigpen converted
into a packing shed for strawberries.

When the strawberry season ended, the older boys went to the canneries up north with our Uncle Ming and Auntie Lily, while my sister Amy, my brother George and I picked beans or did whatever we could find to make some money. Our holiday was a day at the PNE. Going back to school in September was a welcome relief from all the farm work. We enjoyed our schooling, as the students and teachers were always kind to us, but we had very little time to have fun after school or to take part in other activities.

I also remember seeing my father and my brothers David and Ken, digging drainage ditches all around the property that first winter. What a lot of hard, backbreaking labor they went through.

For pets, we had a little, furry, grey Persian cat named Fluffy and a beautiful dog named Rusty — part collie and part German shepherd. The dog loved children and often followed my brother Allan to school, much to the chagrin of Mr. Hawker, the principle of Sunnyside School.

As we were getting accustomed to farm life, misfortune hit hard.

Tragedy!

July 12, 1953 was an unforgettable day. My sister Amy was in the house making lunch, and dad was inside as well, having coffee. The rest of us were in the front yard picking beans. My nine year old little brother Allan, dressed up in his western outfit with his oversized boots on, was in the front yard with a rope playing cowboy while waiting for Auntie Lily, Uncle Ming, and their son Keith to pick him up for a few days visit in Vancouver.

Next thing we knew, my father was yelling for Amy to bring a knife. All of us came running from the bean patch. What I saw next has been etched in my mind ever since. With the rope looped over the veranda railing, Allan was dangling helplessly with more rope wrapped around his neck. A large brass ring dangled on the other end of the rope. My father was furiously trying to cut the rope. When my father finally succeeded in cutting Allan loose, Allan just lay limply in my father's arms not breathing. I remember feeling a faint pulse and hearing Amy say, "Do artificial respiration!" No one knew how to do the complicated procedure which we had only briefly learned at school.

My parents rushed Allan by truck to the nearest hospital — The Royal Columbian Hospital in New Westminster – 30 miles away. On the way, driving up Woodward's Hill, the truck engine burned out. By the time the ambulance arrived and rushed Allan to hospital, he was declared dead on arrival.

Another image etched on my mind was the forlorn, stunned look on my parents face as they exited the police car. The police officer who brought them home declared the incident to be completely accidental.

We later deduced that Allan must have slung the rope over the veranda railing and had tried to pull himself up onto the porch with one foot in the brass ring, which probably slipped off. Wearing those oversized leather boots didn't help. How we, especially my mother and father, got through that horrible time, I'll never know.

Courtesy Family Collection-Allan Morisawa's — graveside-1953

With ripe strawberries still hanging on the plants that summer, the strawberry season ended abruptly for us. My parents had no desire to complete the strawberry season. With heavy hearts, we carried on with weeding, hoeing, fertilizing, and chopping off the tops of the strawberry plants for the remainder of the summer. It was and still is difficult to understand why Allan was taken from us.

However, life had to go on. One winter I remember my father forcing rhubarb indoors. He, the boys, and neighbor Steve Giza, built a cedar shed with large platform shelves inside. A wood stove gave the needed heat. Huge rhubarb roots were hauled in along with dirt to fill in the empty spaces between the roots. The stove produced enough heat to compel the roots to produce stalks indoors. We harvested them after school, bundled the stalks and crated them up in our kitchen till late into the evening. I have never been as exhausted as I was that winter. Luckily, that project of growing indoor rhubarb never did amount to much, and the shed eventually tumbled down.

Life on the farm was a grind. Our teenage years were often spent working until dark. I'm sure we covered every inch of that property many times over. School, homework and work at home left us with little time to pursue any activities of normal teenage life. Having to get back home immediately after school, we were never able to stay for extracurricular activities or sports practices. Many times at school it was not unusual to see one or two Morisawa family members catching up on their sleep in the nurse's room.

My father always had a penchant for business but had failed to make money in his early years. Now having his children to help him, my father was determined to make a go of the farm. He worked hard and had the foresight to grow vegetables to sell until the strawberry plants started producing berries. He also raised pigs and chickens. My father was tough not only on my mother but on us while we were growing up as he had expectations to which we had to live up. He was not always an easy man to please. We often feared my father's harsh, controlling ways, which were probably his way of making sure we didn't get into trouble. (Actually, we didn't have time to get into trouble.)

In spite of these trying times, the years on the farm bonded us as a family. There were many times of laughter around the kitchen table. My father often repeated ghost stories passed on to him by fishermen. We heard about Kasosan's bear from Kelowna. I remember piling on my father's bed in New Denver while my father told those scary stories; my sister Amy cried, but we always asked for more. We enjoyed hearing these stories even into our teenage years.

We often teased my brother George about his crush on a grade five girl at Sunnyside School. Angrily he would chase us all over the strawberry patch.

We found creative ways of making our own fun- playing badminton with makeshift badminton rackets, or playing basketball with the hoop made out of a bucket with the bottom cut out.

A neat place to cool off in the hot summertime was in our swimming hole at the Nicomekl River; where manure floated past us on its way down the current. We rarely made it to the ocean to relax and play.

In many ways life on the farm taught us much about life- how to work hard, be creative, to persevere and to be good Canadian citizens.

After my siblings and I left the farm, and after many years of hard labor and a successful strawberry farm business, my parents' lives improved. The farm prospered, and my mother eventually had a lovely new home to live in built by my two brothers, David and George, and my father. My parents kept working well into my mother's seventieth and my father's eightieth years- planting

Japanese radishes and other vegetables to sell to their friends. They were finally able to enjoy better times in their later years and lived much more comfortably than ever before.

Courtesy Family Collection- Mom and Dad
Morisawa- Enjoying a lighter moment-1980

Other than age-related health problems, my parents had very few worries. They belonged to a poetry club with other Japanese friends, took part in the Japanese United Church bazaars and other related activities in the church.

My family and I are very grateful that my parents were able to enjoy some good times visiting family and traveling before succumbing to the ravages of old age.

Expo '86 came to Vancouver the same year my father turned 88 years old on August 31st, 1986, a special birthday according to Japanese culture. My family and I were thankful we celebrated his birthday and had family pictures taken in the front yard of our Burnaby home. Our family was ill prepared for the changes which soon came upon us. A few months later, in November, my mother had a major stroke and was hospitalized. She was unable to return to her home until she had been rehabilitated adequately in order to care for my father who depended on her heavily. He refused to stay with family and chose to live alone.

I remember one incident that happened while my mother was still in hospital. There was a power outage when my Auntie Lily and I went to Surrey to check on my father. We scrambled to find candles and flashlight batteries. Eventually the lights came back on, but the water pump in the basement failed to work. Being city folk, my Auntie Lily and I had no idea how to prime a water pump. We had no choice but to bring my father down the stairs. My Auntie Lily on one side, me on the other, and my father in his bathrobe and slippers hobbling slowly down the stairs to the basement, one step at a time. We finally got him down, and my father primed the pump. We managed to get him back upstairs again without incident, but what a comical sight we must have been, an old man in his bathrobe and two city-slicker women heading downstairs to prime a water pump.

Living alone for that short time, my father's health soon began to fail. Eventually he was hospitalized for respiratory, diabetic, and other health related problems.

My father passed away on February 19, 1987. In the spring of 1988, the Mulroney government passed legislation making a token financial compensation to the Japanese Canadians for their losses during their evacuation from the west coast of British Columbia. They also acknowledged and made a formal apology for the injustices suffered by the Japanese Canadians. I thought of the hardships, the adjustments, and the trials and tribulations my parents experienced during the war. I cried and felt saddened that my father didn't live to hear the apology from the Canadian government or to receive the token monetary compensation.

Although he struggled in his early years, my father had a great determination to make the farm a success. With the help of his family the land was transformed from raw land to a beautiful strawberry farm. His vision and determination to run a successful farm business greatly benefitted my siblings and I in ensuing years. He left us a legacy of hard work that we will never forget.

Following the passing of my father, my hemiplegic mother with remarkable resilience and adaptability chose to live alone on the farm with help from family and neighbors.

After seven years, circumstances necessitated her to move to our home in Burnaby. We got to know my mother in a different way. We could see traces of impishness which remained in her. We always had a good laugh at her antics. Her favorite antic was pushing her suitcase down the stairs. As she enjoyed visiting other family members she would pack her suitcase days ahead. When the time came for her to leave, on a couple occasions we heard something tumbling down the stairs. Expecting to see her lying at the bottom of the stairs injured or unconscious, we went flying to see what happened. What a relief it was to see my mother standing and laughing at the top of the stairs. Being just a tiny lady (barely five feet tall) with a huge infectious smile and a hearty laugh, it was difficult to get annoyed with her. Whether she was trying to be helpful or just being mischievous, or a combination of the two, she certainly enjoyed getting a reaction out of us.

My mother entertained us with stories of her childhood exploits and always looked for little chores to do around the house, especially the laundry. Every evening at 5 pm sharp, she would have the rice steaming in the rice cooker. My husband said that he enjoyed eating rice, "but not every single day."

What a privilege it was to have her in our home the short time she lived with us. She especially enjoyed my late husband Mats who had a way of making her laugh with his sense of humor. I am so grateful to Mats who did things for Mom over and beyond what any son-in-law was expected to do. He was always patient and kind while he helped transport my mother around and good naturedly did whatever he could to help my mother.

A memorable vacation was a family cruise to Alaska. One morning I asked my mother if she would like to go on a train ride or a helicopter ride as a side trip that day. She quickly replied, "A helicopter ride." Fortunate to get a helicopter that had a hydraulic lift that could take her into the cabin, my mother was soon to take the ride of her lifetime. It was an amazing ride flying close to the base of the pristine white glaciers with its unbelievable icy grey shadowy formations. An azure blue sky framed the beautiful glaciers. It was a spectacular sight. My mother grinned from ear to ear the entire time. When we landed on one of the glaciers and we got out to walk on the icy blue glacial surface, she, of course, stayed in the helicopter but she never stopped grinning. None of us knew that taking a helicopter or a small plane ride was one of her lifelong dreams. When we arrived home in Burnaby she told family, "Now I can die."

It was soon after that trip that I'll never forget the morning my mother was found on the floor beside her bed, delirious with high fever from an infected leg wound. She needed to be hospitalized. That incident marked the beginning of further deterioration of my mother's health. After a fall, my mother fractured her right hip and needed surgery. Following rehabilitation, she still needed more care than we could give her. My mother was admitted to the Fellburn Private Hospital close to our Burnaby home. She accepted the move with much grace and adapted quickly to her new abode.

I visited nearly every day and as soon as she saw me, her face would break into a huge smile. My siblings also visited from out of town. Pushing herself in her wheelchair with her good leg, she would lead the way down the hall to her room. Due to her stroke in 1986 and several small strokes since, she had difficulty speaking. Even with her aphasia she animatedly endeavored to tell me of the events of the day and the people who visited, especially whenever "the pilot" grandson, Philip, had dropped in.

My mother enjoyed field trips, playing Bingo or doing wheelchair square dancing which she loved. My mother made it so easy for us to visit her, never complaining or asking to return to our home. She remained quite content in the nursing home.

When my mother eventually passed away there in the nursing home in 1998, her doctor summed up her last years aptly: "Your mom was a very special, unique lady. She was able to bounce back from all her difficulties and able to keep on smiling. It was a joy to visit her."

Even now, whenever I drive past the hospital, I can picture my mother sitting waiting for me at the entrance and breaking out into her huge smile as she greeted me. I agree with the doctor's assessment of my mother, Naoye.

We are also grateful to my parents for their hard work, diligence, endurance, and their sacrificial love on our behalf.

Memories of "blood, sweat and tears" on the farm became years of fond recollections of being bonded together as family. We remain a close family to this day. When the farm sold many years later, I didn't realize how attached I had become to that place. Nostalgia mixed with a sense of relief that the farm finally sold and some sadness that my parents weren't around to enjoy the fruit of their labors, flooded my mind as I took final pictures of the farm. I also thought how my own grandchildren would have enjoyed the wide open spaces running around picking berries and riding with my father on his red tractor.

Life After The Farm

Because family expressed interest in adding information about our lives after the farm, here are submissions from family members regarding their perspectives of life both on the farm and after high school. I am thankful they have shared their experiences, as I was unaware of so many interesting aspects of their lives which followed after leaving the farm.

My late sister Diane was spared working on the farm as she was already in Vancouver before we returned to the coast. Because she passed away in 2005 before this story was written, her daughter-in- law, Irene Iwata, has submitted a summary of Diane's life.

Diana Kiyono Iwata

(nee Morisawa)

born March 24 1932

Courtesy Family Collection- Diane (Morisawa) Iwata

Diana Kiyono Morisawa was born in Kelowna, B.C. on March 24th, 1932. She was the oldest child born to Kanekichi and Naoye Morisawa.

Diana and her family were evacuated from Victoria BC, to Hastings Park and then to a relocation camp in New Denver during the war. After the war ended, she and her family lived in Slocan and then in Silverton. She quit high school early to help her parents work at the Enterprise Mining Company. It was there she met a young man and became pregnant. Her parents sent her to Vancouver BC to go to Business College where she lived with her Auntie Lily and Uncle Ming Mah and worked in the Mah family store. There in a Vancouver hospital she gave birth to her baby girl. Diana gave her baby up for adoption to a mixed race couple. The Aida's were a Japanese man with a Caucasian wife.

After receiving her business degree, Diana began working in a company dealing with import and export of pulp products and machinery, called CT Takahashi & Co. with offices in Japan and Seattle, Washington. It was at work that she met a very handsome man named Tom Iwata who worked for the Seattle office and knew Diana would be the one he would marry.

Diana converted to Catholicism and soon Tom and Diana married at St. Mary's Church in Spokane, Washington in November 1953. They honeymooned in California. They first lived in an apartment and soon began having children. Stanley was born in 1954 and David in 1955.

They moved to their new home on Beacon Hill where Andrew was born in 1956, Gordon in 1957, Ann in 1959, Roger in 1960 and Jeff in 1964. Diane loved babies. With such a large family she managed to show great love for all. Her fourth son Gordon especially treasures the day he had her all to himself for the whole day and couldn't believe they were doing something without the rest of the kids.

Tom, Diana and the kids often visited her parents and the family on the farm in Surrey. There were many happy family celebrations there in ensuing years. Over the years their older boys often came to help Grandpa Morisawa on the farm — driving the little red tractor, picking berries, etc. After Diana's parents had their new home, Tom, Diana and the boys helped pull down the old shack that her family first lived in. Each time they visited there were so many chores they were able to do to help their parents. Diana was fortunate to have a husband so skilled in many ways.

Andy, the third son recalls, "Mom always had a great sense of humor. One day on a crabbing trip Diana spotted a huge crab and called to the kids to come look. The kids all came over making the boat lean. Diana fell over the side of the boat. When she surfaced and they all realized that the water was very shallow, Diana started to laugh, much to the relief of all the kids who joined in the laughter."

One time when I (Irene) was there for the evening, I went to the bathroom and found the water all the way to the top of the toilet bowl. So I told Diana who went into the bathroom and she was going to plunge the toilet when all of a sudden water shot out of the toilet bowl right into her face. I screamed and Tom came running. Diana got out of the water spray and began to laugh. Tom turned off the water and set off to do the repair. Oldest son, Stan agrees she had a great sense of humor and a wonderful laugh.

Diana was a magnificent cook and always the gracious hostess. The Iwata home was always full of kids and Japanese visitors. Diana had a way of making everyone feel at home and would provide them with their favorite foods. "Momma Iwata's famous lasagna" or "beef stroganoff" was among the many delicious dishes everyone enjoyed.

Her husband Tom was always hosting business visitors or exchange students from Japan, which meant Diana was often cooking and traveling around to different Washington or Canadian tourist spots to show her visitors and her kids around.

Diana was a night owl; she stayed up late in the night getting things done, like cleaning and laundry. She would get a second burst of energy after the children went to bed and start baking. She was a great baker, something she learned at the mine from her dad. She learned to get up early to prepare bread dough for the miners.

With children growing up, Diana joined the work force. She worked at Sears Roebuck in the mail order department doing data entry for many years. Eventually with layoffs and the closing of the department, she retired from Sears.

After retirement Diana wanted to own several of her own businesses. One of which was the Muffin Break which was opened in 1989.

In the three years she owned it, she had a very successful clientele. She loved to supplement the menu with fruits and vegetables from her own garden. She discovered it was difficult to hire good dependable help. But Stan says," She often went in at two in the morning because a baker wouldn't show up, and then work till ten pm." Eventually two of her sons, Roger and Jeff were hired and proved to be great bakers.

In the third year after opening her store, Diana discovered she had diabetes. It had been undetected for some time, and her kidneys were significantly damaged. She decided to sell the Muffin Break and made a good profit. Diana never sat still long and soon she embarked on the Jenny Craig program, lost weight, and began exercising. She attended line-dancing classes, walked at the mall, and attended other exercise classes.

Diana had other avocations as well. She enjoyed traveling abroad and visited Japan, Singapore, Thailand, and London and went on cruises to Alaska and the Caribbean. She and Tom traveled to China with son Andy and family to pick up her new granddaughter, Claire. Of course, she visited many places in the US and

Canada. She enjoyed the many family outings, including hunting for matsutake mushrooms and picking huckleberries. And always there was a hot pot of chili and hot chocolate milk to go with them on these outings.

She attended an investment class and became an investor herself. She tried to interest each of her children in it by gifting them an investment fund.

Maggie, Diana's daughter whom she gave up for adoption tells of meeting Diana.

> Well, I guess my story would be about meeting Mom. I got a call from the adoption registry only a few weeks after filing all the forms. I was told that Mom was married with 7 children and living in Seattle. It was arranged that Mom would call me on a certain day. So I waited for her call wondering what it was going to be like to really talk to her and maybe meet her. It was a wonderful first visit on the phone. She asked if she and Tom could come up to meet me and my family. So we arranged a day and I waited in anticipation for the moment to finally meet her. Right away Tom said it was no mistake that I was her daughter; he saw a resemblance. It was a beautiful spring day and we spent the afternoon having lunch and visiting. We all went out for dinner and they asked if we would like to meet the rest of the family. Shortly thereafter I received these beautiful notes and pictures from all my siblings. I treasure them to this day. A few weeks later we were honored with an incredible family gathering in Seattle. I was so grateful to be welcomed by all of them. It is very special for my children and grandchildren also to enjoy this family connection.

Diana managed her diabetes very well and it was not until 2002 that her kidneys began to fail requiring her to consider dialysis. She resisted the whole process and wound up in the Intensive Care Unit with fluid overload because her kidneys were not getting rid of it fast enough. But even from her hospital bed, Diana was concerned about her children. Stan was ill and Diana wanted him to seek more medical care. She was not worried about herself but about him. After her fluid situation was corrected, she began to prepare for dialysis. Her kidneys began to fail rapidly and she was feeling very ill when her peritoneal catheter was placed. In spite of many attempts to get her dialysis started, it did not begin until she went to her post-operative appointment when the surgeon contacted her nephrologist telling him that she needed to start dialysis immediately as she was quite ill.

Arrangements were made, but tragically the night before she was to begin, her heart rate dropped to 28 beats per minute. Her blood pressure medication, which should have been decreased due to her kidney failure, became toxic. With such a slow heart rate and by the time she got to the emergency room and oxygen was provided, Diana suffered anoxia and unbeknownst to the family, brain damage. She received her dialysis during that hospital stay and there was no evidence of any problems.

For over two years, Diana remained on peritoneal dialysis with extensive help from her husband and children. She was able to attend family reunions and travel to visit family in Canada. She was able to pass on bits and pieces of her memories as she performed her daily dialysis. I was grateful for time spent together as she was able to teach me how to be a better cook. Diana got to meet and carry her last grandchild, Madison, born to youngest son Jeff and his wife Lisa. Tom and Diana celebrated 50 years of marriage in 2003. They were able to gather with friends and family to celebrate their lives together.

Her daughter, Ann felt it was a blessing that Mom was able to remember the bigger events that happened in her last years, even though she had a greatly diminished short-term memory. She was able to enjoy these memories, such as their 50th wedding anniversary, and the happy times with family, friends and especially her grandchildren.

Eventually Diana's circulation began shutting down in her legs causing her great pain and then gangrene in her feet. She became bedridden and required 24 hours care. On May 10, 2005, two days after the whole family gathered and celebrated Mother's Day, Diana passed away. But Diana left a legacy.

Diana was dedicated to family and friends. To Tom, she was a loving and devoted wife. To her children, she was a caring mother and role model. To her extended family, she was a wonderful sister, aunt, cousin and mother-in-law. As a host, she always made any friends or guests of her children welcome in her home. For many years, her children would invite their friends to the traditional Japanese New Year's Day open house.

Diana took her mothering responsibilities seriously. She taught her children the value of honest work and responsibility. She assigned chores to all the children, and weekends included some sort of family work party. As teenagers, they all had jobs, were expected to pay for some of their expenses, and a portion of any earnings were set aside for education.

She never pushed her advice on her children as adults nor interfered in their married lives. She showed much discretion in showing concern for her children.

As mentioned earlier, Diana had a well-deserved reputation as an accomplished cook, and many of her dishes became family favorites. For Diana, cooking was a caring expression to family and friends. Her meals epitomized home cooking in traditional Japanese and American foods. Dinnertime was her way to bring the family together at least once a day. She was strict about the family not wasting food by making sure they ate everything on their plates. She also made sure her family ate healthy. Her son Jeff doesn't remember having fast foods very often.

Diana enjoyed participating in cooking with her children, especially her daughter Ann with whom it was a tradition making sushi together for their annual traditional New Years' Day feast. Ann misses and cherished those times together.

Diana kept a close family. Together they did so many things together — huckleberry picking, mushroom picking, crabbing, and fishing. To this day her children continue these activities with their own families.

Education was important to Diana. She spent many hours with her children, beginning with teaching them to read. Through the school years she helped type papers in the middle of the night, tutored and quizzed, and always discussed the necessity of a good education. Tom and Diana raised their children in the Catholic faith. . Her children attended Catholic elementary and high schools. Although Diana was discrete with expressing her beliefs, they were demonstrated through her living example and strong convictions.

Diana took special joy in her 10 grandchildren; she was always interested to hear of their latest exploits. Pictures were many and stories were always shared with friends and family. Grandchildren filled the Iwata home at frequent family gatherings and were doted on with Easter egg hunts as well as baskets full of goodies, Christmas craft parties, and mochi- making and sushi-rolling at New Years. Diana always sent birthday cards and gifts to each of her children, their spouses and grandchildren.

Diana always loved gardening, and devoted more time to her avocations when the children were grown. She attended classes, becoming a Master Gardener. Diana then used her horticultural knowledge to help with various workshops, as well as volunteering at Kubota Gardens. There is evidence at the Iwata home today of her gardening skills.

Diana will always be remembered for her love of plants, her cooking, baking, and gardening but mostly for her love and care of us whom she loved and loved her.

David Tokudo Morisawa

born April 24, 1933

Courtesy Private Collection- David

Firstly, I am going to summarize my life since leaving Silverton B.C. in the fall of 1949 to the life on the West coast.

In July and August 1949 I stayed behind in Silverton keeping busy packing and canning peaches, while the rest of the family had gone to make money in the Okanagan picking hops for our planned move to Surrey. I remember having a terrible allergic rash that was so itchy and sore. Dad had already bought a 15 acre farm in Surrey, B.C.

I was in grade ten when we moved in mid-September to our farm in Surrey via the Greyhound bus and settled in the shack- like house which needed lots of repairs. There was a long two- story chicken house, outhouse, barn, and pig pen shed. Steve Giza was our bachelor neighbor with a five acre farm. Dad bought a 1941 Chevrolet pick-up truck and got driving lessons from Steve. I enrolled at Semiahmoo High School, along with Ken and Amy, while Sumi and George went to Sunnyside Elementary School. Mainly Ken and I worked hard to help clear the land to farm in the spring. We had to make and store firewood in the barn for cooking and heating. Dad used to go to Cloverdale frequently to buy feed for the broiler chickens. The large building housed around 100 chickens which were mostly sold at an auction, but we kept some for ourselves. I learned to chop off the chicken heads with a hatchet and soak them in very hot water, so their feathers could be pulled off cleanly. We also raised six big pigs from small piglets. Mother had a knack in rounding them up by banging on the metal feed pail when they escaped from the pen. Occasionally one or two were slaughtered and stored in a rented, cold storage for our meat supply.

Dad decided to raise strawberry plants in a small cleared area to start with. To help our survival, Uncle Ming got Ken and me a job in a fish cannery in Butedale, B.C. With our earnings we managed to make the annual farm payment plus help with living expenses until the first berry harvest came the following spring.

Every summer we worked in the fish cannery up north until I graduated from Semiahmoo in 1952. I helped on the farm for the next two years, and Dad bought the 1.78 acres adjoining land from Steve Giza to make our land a total of 16.78 acres. By this time we learned how to dynamite tree stumps to expand land for farming. The large fir tree windfalls were good for firewood, but cutting it up with a 6-foot crosscut saw to stove length was exhausting and time consuming. Never have I seen Mom so angry and scared as the day a stump blast went off from a large piece of root 300 feet from our house and landed on the edge of our roof near the kitchen. Luckily she was not hurt, but swore a lot at Dad. We found large first growth cedar windfalls, ideal as shakes for the roof and sides of the rhubarb shed we built, which we also used for raising mushrooms with horse manure as base.

It's a wonder I didn't suffocate tending the oil barrel stove fire to keep the shed temperature up all night. Both crops did not amount to much and the shed stood idle for some years, when it finally collapsed on its own.

The strawberry plants flourished and we harvested bumper crops after three to four years. This is due to the huge amounts of whatever pig, mink or chicken manure we could get for free to spread on the plants during fall and winter. I made sure that at night I washed thoroughly in our washtub bath, so no odor was present at school.

After my high school graduation ceremony, I took Ann Skelton to the after-grad party in our 1941 Chevrolet truck. I had to clean it twice to get rid of the manure smell. Unfortunately, Ann passed away soon after high school from an unknown sickness. This reminds me: We did not have any health insurance, but somehow, luckily, we all stayed fairly healthy. We drank the well water located 10 feet from the creek alongside the house for over 20 years, until the city water finally got piped in, with which I helped.

For my own future I enrolled at Vancouver Vocational Institute to learn a trade in building construction. I apprenticed with Narod Construction Co. on job sites like the George Massey Tunnel, Richmond Municipal Building, and various residential houses. Unfortunately, I had to return to V.V.I. to learn another trade, as I had to get an operation on my right knee for cartilage removal, which ended my building trade ambition. I did get an electrical/electronic job to apprentice as an aircraft avionic technician with Canada Pacific Airlines. Later I worked for the Canadian Airlines.

36 years later I retired in November 1997 from my last job as Airline Maintenance Planner.

My brother Allan was just nine years old when he died from a tragic accident in 1953. When my brother George was just finishing high school, he gave me lots of help building Mom and Dad's house. My short experience in carpentry came in handy as I built the new family house with salvaged timber from the burnt White Rock pier and other secondhand and new building materials. I gained tremendous experience too. I read lots of books on electrical wiring, plumbing, gyproc installations, etc . — all within the building code, since we had to get inspections passed for each building stage. I had good results in getting everything passed. George Sasaki (his son Roger married cousin Sandi many years later) built the brick chimney for us, for which we were very grateful. I did not want to attempt it myself in case of fire hazards.

I chuckle at some of the moments I recall, which were quite comical and unusual scenarios, like, George flying out from the outhouse with a lit cigarette in his boot when he saw Dad coming towards him (George's last smoking experiment); Amy and Sumi in their red snowsuits, picking up wood chips from the farm berry patch, one pushing and the other pulling on a rope tied to the wheelbarrow; myself getting knocked head over heels after discharging a double barrel shot gun to scare off a herd of deer eating strawberry plants. (Luckily, I was wearing a quilted jacket to cushion the recoil from the gun.) After a while I learned to brace myself by practicing shooting at the outhouse target, which by now was well ventilated. We fooled around with blasting caps and dynamite.

George and I had to re-roof the second story of the chicken house. We tied ourselves with heavy rope to the roof peak and carried probably twenty rolls of roofing up a shaky wooden extension ladder. I still shudder in wonder how we did not fall or hurt ourselves.

There are many stories, including Ken's old car, a Skoda, in which he drove back across Canada. It was finally laid to rest forever in the corner of the berry field.

The family move to Surrey, I think, turned out to be the right one, as I, especially, gained a tremendous amount of experience: had the opportunity to help run the farm, do the farm accounts and income tax and even keep the farm status long after Dad and Mom passed on. I had to work with all the possible ways to keep it a farm operation until we finally sold it in 2005. The stroke of luck was that the farm was leased for two years to Tak Yamanaka, who raised nursery trees on the land, and when the lease expired he left behind 200 trees which we took ownership of. Therefore, we became nursery operators entitled to a "farm operations" designation for property taxes and income tax purposes. It took quite a bit of effort to convince the tax assessor to keep this status, for which I had to reapply every three years.

We are thankful that Dad had not sold the farm property earlier when he was tempted many times by real estate agents and developers who knocked at the door. He knew that the land was much more valuable than what buyers were willing to offer him, so the property remained unsold long after he passed away and even after Mom left the farm. The farm was left for us as an inheritance. So even through hardship, with luck and experience, moving to Surrey was a good thing.

In 1965 when I started my last job as airline Maintenance Planner, it was a very busy year. I was successful in getting a full time avionics position after completing my apprenticeship with CPA in February.

I met Taeko Uematsu the previous fall of 1964 at the Renfrew United Church. That winter was cold, and we had an unusual record snowfall. Going out on dates was difficult because my '57 Ford Meteor kept sliding and getting stuck everywhere we went.

At the end of March 1965 we decided to get married. Our children are Naomi (1967) and Philip (1970). Naomi married Alan and gave us two grandchildren: Bobby and Mira. Philip's wife Denise gave us granddaughter Gemma. We love and enjoy them all very much. I am happily married 48 years now, retired for fourteen years and very active, traveling countries of the world, volunteering in Lions Club, ESS (Emergency Social Services) and member of Pt. Roberts Golf club. I am blessed to do as I please each day, and am very grateful for good health with just a touch of diabetes.

Kenneth Moritsugu Morisawa

born October 12, 1934

Courtesy Private Collection- Ken

I worked at various mining jobs to earn enough money to complete university after I left the farm. The mining jobs were a bit of an adventure geographically because they were in very remote locations-starting in the Northwest Territories and finishing in Tilt Cove, Newfoundland -as far as you can go!

My first job was as a lab technician at Ray Rock Mines, north of Yellowknife, NT. I did the testing or assays on the uranium or yellow cake before it was shipped to Port Hope, Ontario. This mine was so primitive it didn't even have a ping pong table — the main recreation was gambling, mostly poker. You had to stay at least a year to get your way paid in and out, but that was all you could stand!

The next stop was Sudbury, Ontario, where the real uranium mining boom was happening. However, as luck would have it, a flood at one of the biggest mines in the region put so many miners out of work; we had to move to the next uranium mining area — Bancroft, Ontario. After laying track underground, something I wasn't exactly suited for and not exactly profitable, I decided to move on.

My final stop was at Maritime Mining Co., a copper mine located on the northeast corner of NL named Tilt Cove. You have not lived unless you have spent a winter on this cold windswept former fishing village! My job as a base metal assayer working 12-hour shifts was ideal for saving money, and the time flew by quickly. The camp was a bit more civilized with a well-funded recreation club, which I ran with a mill foreman from South Africa.

After university I worked at various accounting and financial jobs, everything from toy and clothing manufacturing to the air pollution control business in Toronto. Some of the jobs were interesting and challenging, others dull and boring.

My main recreation while in Toronto was tennis, and I played at a number of tennis clubs. I finally ended up at a small club where I helped organize tournaments, gave group lessons, played in league competitions, organized various social events, and took turns running the club. People still talk about the parties we had and the number of people who met and married each other as a result of belonging to the club. Of course, Sheila and I met at the club, and we still have a number of friends who were members.

1977 was a landmark year because Sheila Reid and I got married, got jobs and settled down in Georgetown and started the construction of our own tennis court (talk about priorities)! We started in

1978 and finished in 1979 after a lot of help from our friends from the club in Toronto. Son Christopher arrived in 1981 and the next 15 years were busy taking him to lessons, drills, and tournaments. Chris lives in North Vancouver and works in Vancouver. Other activities in the last 33 years were taken up by a major renovation to our house, putting in a Japanese garden complete with pond, stream, waterfall and Japanese koi, a vegetable garden, and other landscaping endeavors.

Since retirement we have spent part of every winter in Florida, travelled to Vienna and Salzburg, Austria; Nagaoka, Kyoto, and Wakayama, Japan. Chris was teaching English at the time of our visit to Japan and toured with us. The highlight of our trip was a visit to the village of Mio in the Wakayama, prefecture where Dad was born and where the Morisawa home still exists. Other cities we have travelled to are Chicago, Illinois, and Tanglewood, Massachusetts in the US and Joliette, Quebec and of course, to Vancouver to visit Chris.

I keep busy with maintaining our property, photography, attending concerts, and listening to music. I thank God for my good health, my wife Sheila, my son Christopher, and our belief in Jesus Christ and our Catholic faith.

Amy Morisawa Chan

(nee Morisawa)

born August 22, 1936

Courtesy Private Collection- Amy

Life on the Farm:

As I remember, life on the farm was hardly fun. We all worked together as a family to help Dad cultivate the virgin timbered acreage into a successful and yielding farm. From sunrise to sundown, physical work was the everyday norm. Aside from making a living on strawberries (which yielded once a year), Dad had the foresight to grow other crops like corn, tomatoes, spinach, etc., that he would take on the truck and sell to residents in White Rock for cash. With the cash, he would buy meat, milk, and butter for the family. He worked hard physically, and every morning he would get up with an aching back and mom would have to get a hot water bottle to soothe his ache. Mom had physical problems, too, but never discussed her aches and pains — she was too busy taking care of all of us. She suffered from high blood pressure for years but never had the chance to monitor it correctly; it is a wonder that she was as healthy as she was until her stroke at 78 years old.

I remember sitting in the field late in the evening thinking of life after the farm. When I graduated from high school, what were my goals? To leave the farm and get as far away as possible was my first priority. How? Attending UBC and majoring in pharmacy was my first intention. But with five children who needed educating, there was no way for Mom and Dad to help with schooling.

In my senior year at Semiahmoo, I applied and was fortunate to get 3 scholarships. After working the summer as a sorter in a fish cannery in New Westminster, along with the scholarships, I had enough funds to pay for tuition and dormitory fees at UBC and enough left over to buy myself a purple winter coat.

UBC was a bewildering place. After attending a small school in White Rock with limited social experience, I felt lost and confused on the campus. All the students seemed well adjusted and had mutual friends to study with and to attend football games and movies with. My roommate Charlotte was only an acquaintance; she was a popular basketball player who dated Bob Langlands. She was gone most of the time with Bob so it was quite lonely, especially on Friday and Saturday nights. It was also very lonely academically; Mom & Dad had me on a high pedestal since I did well in school and had won three scholarships to UBC! I tried hard to get good grades in my first year at university and wanted to be worthy of the scholarships that were awarded to me. I didn't get exceptional grades my first year, but I only managed to pass with an average grade, which disappointed me greatly.

To continue at UBC, I had to have funds from other sources. My intent was to work as a pharmacy intern after my first year and then continue working to pay for my classes toward a bachelor of science. Well, it did not work out that way. I interviewed at Rexall Drugs, Owl Drugs, and other firms for internship. I was turned down for the positions at each interview- perhaps being an Asian female in a male dominated field had much bearing.

After searching for an alternative to pharmacy, I saw an ad for science majors who were interested in laboratory technology. The pathologist at Royal Columbian Hospital in New Westminster explained the program, and since it paid a stipend to train as a technologist, I jumped at the opportunity to take this 24- month course. I lived in Vancouver with a doctor and his wife and their two children, and in exchange for room and board, I was their occasional babysitter/nanny. I traveled from Vancouver to New Westminster by bus (one hour trip) for one year while in this training. Fortunately, I was able to complete this 24 month course in 18 months, so I started full salary as a laboratory technologist in 1957.

From 1957-1958 I worked at local hospitals in White Rock and Langley. Then from 1958-1959 I attended the University of Alberta majoring in hematology. There I obtained specialty certification in hematology.

Then from 1959-1961 I attended the University of Hawaii and majored in Biological Science. I obtained my Bachelor of Science degree in 1961 after which I left the university. I then married Peter Chan and settled in Southern California.

There I worked as a lab technologist for four years and eventually became Chief technologist. By the time I retired in 1992 I was the Laboratory Administrator.

We have three children and four grandchildren. We have lived on a two acre avocado farm in north San Diego County for the past 10 years. My husband Peter purchased an out-of-business restaurant property in 1969 and refurbished it into a large restaurant serving both Chinese and American cuisine. Its lounge and banquet facilities served both the public and Santa Fe Springs' city employees. He also owned and managed two other facilities: a Mexican restaurant in Norwalk, CA, and a steak and seafood restaurant in Whittier, CA. From 1983 to 1992 Peter owned and operated public pay telephones along with coin operated water dispensing equipment. From 1992 to the present, Peter has managed his real estate investment portfolio.

Sumi Kinoshita

(nee Morisawa)

born February 22, 1938

Courtesy Private Collection — Sumi

Forty-six years of marriage ended for me on June 13th, 2008 when my husband Matsu slipped into God's presence after an eight month courageous battle with cancer and treatments. This was a major turn of events for me after a wonderful life with my husband and one of the most difficult experiences of my life. We had no idea he would live less than eight months after moving to our new condominium.

Following high school I attended one year at Prairie Bible School, three years at Vancouver General Hospital's school of nursing, then attended another year of Bible school at Vancouver Bible College.

Having accepted Jesus Christ as my personal Savior at the age of 15 at an evangelistic rally in White Rock, I had a strong compulsion to attend church and Young Peoples meetings whenever I could. My brother, sister and I had been exposed to the Bible at a Sunday school held in Jack and Erma William's home several years earlier.

Being misunderstood by my family and schoolmates was something I didn't expect as a new Christian. During those days, Christians didn't go to movies, wear makeup, dance, play cards, or drink alcohol. My carefree life during the evacuation years ended when we moved to the farm and our parents needed the help of the whole family to run the farm. Life as a farm girl was pretty difficult and dull, but becoming a Christian didn't make matters any better.

Also as a fifth born, I never felt very important in the family. I hated hand-me-down clothes, and most of all I resented being compared to my older sister and expected to be like her. Feelings of rejection led to discouragement. I had many conflicts with my parents, especially my father, whom I had a difficult time pleasing.

I chose to go to Bible School in an unknown place called Three Hills in the back hills of Alberta. (They were actually just three bumps in the horizon.) I was pretty naïve about the Japanese way of thinking where conformity is the norm. To have a child who makes the unusual choice of going to Bible school against her parents' wishes must have caused my parents to "lose face." No wonder my father was furious at my decision. The idea of going to a Bible school was totally foreign to my parents and certainly not an ideal way of getting an education. They could not understand why I was not going into nursing as I had originally planned. How would it ever contribute to earning a living? I later appreciated my father's legitimate concerns for my wellbeing. My relationship with him improved when I did go into nursing, matured, got married and had children of my own.

I wondered whether God was calling me to the mission field. Going to Bible School was a good place to find out as well as to discover what Christianity was all about. After a year at Bible School, I felt called to enter nurse's training. Nursing was a great place for this country hick to learn how to take care of herself as well as others. I met wonderful, lifelong friends with whom I had much in common.

It was near the end of my nurses' training that I met my husband Matsu through a Japanese ministry. We got married in 1962, two years after I graduated. We had two daughters, Ruth and Karen. I worked a couple years each at Burnaby General Hospital and Vancouver General Hospital before and after marriage, and then worked in nursing occasionally while raising my family. When the girls were older, I returned to work part time as a Home Care Nurse for fifteen years with the Burnaby Health Department. I really loved that work, but with having rheumatoid arthritis, I wasn't able to work as long as I would have liked.

We were privileged to have Tenth Ave Alliance as our church family for 36 years. There my husband and I were able to continue our passion for serving God and raising our daughters in a church context. How grateful we were for the great Bible teaching and Christian fellowship we enjoyed at Tenth Ave. Alliance Church. I also spent many years in Bible Study Fellowship, an international nondenominational Bible study group which provided another venue for learning God's word and serving Him. It was a great place to learn some leadership skills and to meet new friends.

It's hard to believe that I was so blessed with a wonderful husband, family, friends, and a career and traveling beyond my expectations. I was also thankful for the improved relationships with my parents as my faith in God grew, I could accept myself as I was. Knowing God loved me as I was gave me confidence in being myself and in pursuing my own passions.

I've spent my whole life as a British Columbian and always lived within driving distance of my parents on the farm helping to look after them. My husband Mats and I lived in Burnaby for 33 years. We built a new home in Coquitlam and after 5 years living there, we moved into the condominium I now live in. Unfortunately Mats passed away eight months after moving in.

While my mother was away visiting family, her house was vandalized, so upon return, she moved in with us. Mats and I were privileged to take care of her in our Burnaby home and later in nearby Fellburn Private Hospital where she spent her last days.

Participating with my brother Dave in the sale of the farm was an adventure in itself. After ten years of meetings with city hall, realtors and family, we were successful in selling our beloved farm in 2005.

Widowed for over five years now, I am adjusting to a single lifestyle. I enjoy walking, fitness, swimming and dabbling in some art lessons. Volunteering at church in the women's and senior's groups and learning a new racket sport called pickleball keep me busy. I am so grateful for many friends and family and opportunities to travel. In spite of my arthritis, I am grateful to be able to do almost everything I want.

My two daughters live nearby with their families. Ruth with her two sons-Timothy and Kyle, live in Port Moody, BC. Karen and her husband David, have 3 children-Matthew, Hannah and Rachel. They live in Coquitlam BC.

George Morisawa

born June 22, 1939

Courtesy Private Collection- George

During World War II, I was only two years old and I was spared the horrific memories of having our family abruptly torn from our house and shipped out of Victoria to the transition station of Hastings Park, Vancouver and ultimately to the internment camp in New Denver BC.

During the internment, because I was a child, I was unaware of the hardships my parents and family experienced. After the war, we moved to Slocan BC and then to Silverton BC. My parents and oldest sister, Diane worked as cooks at the Enterprise Mine. They worked hard and saved their money to eventually have a better life for their family.

I was six years old when we moved to Silverton, and I have fond memories of Silverton. We lived in a beautiful setting on the Slocan Lake in the Rocky Mountains. People of Silverton were very kind to us; we felt very little discrimination, especially when we had friends like Betty and Gordie Nelson, the Barry Morrison family and Georgie Nelson's family. In Silverton, I attended elementary school and all I did was play. I depended on my older brothers and sisters to manage our lives. Mom and Dad would come down from the mine to see us from time to time.

In 1949 we moved to South Surrey, BC where Mom and Dad had bought land with an old farmhouse on it. My sister Diane helped us buy the farm with the money she had saved from working at the Enterprise Mine. Later Diane went to live in Vancouver where she worked as a secretary for a Japanese firm. For a time, my sisters Amy and Sumi and I stayed with our aunt and uncle, Tomichan (Auntie Lily) and Uncle Ming. Uncle Ming gave David and Ken a chance to work in the canneries to help Dad pay off the farm. Tomichan has always been gracious and humble regarding all the help she has given our family in so many ways, and she has never changed her style. She is such a classy lady!

The farm is where the real work began. Huge Douglas fir stumps had to be blasted and split so the bulldozers could make a huge pile of wood that would burn all winter long. Spring came and the land had to be plowed and planted in strawberries. Along the way, there were many hardships while trying to make a living off the land, but with hard work it became a beautiful strawberry farm.

We worked hard on the farm, but we also had light hearted moments. At night after work we shot hoops through a bucket (with the bottom cut out) attached to the barn with the barn lights on. When I had a crush on Paula Moore, Sumi and Amy teased the heck out of me about it, and I would chase them all over the strawberry patch. As I look back on my life on the farm, I realize the experience taught me integrity, morals, team work, and how to be a good, hardworking citizen. I feel this is the legacy my parents left our family.

I was 14-years-old when tragedy struck our family. My younger brother Allan died in a terrible accident at the age of nine. His death affected me deeply, and I couldn't understand or forgive God for taking such a young, innocent child away from us. To this day, I still miss Allan, my younger brother.

I attended Sunnyside Elementary School and Semiahmoo High School. During high school I had friends, but I was lucky to have a good friend, Jimmy Rodgers. I will always be grateful to Jimmy and his family for the friendship they extended to me. Many times his mom would leave a plate on the dinner table just in case I might drop in unexpectedly for dinner. When I stayed over at Jimmy's house, Jimmy's dad would get us up early the next morning, make breakfast for us, and then make sure I left for home so I could go to work on the farm and not get into trouble.

I graduated from high school in 1957. I then attended post-graduate school for a short time to be an accountant, but not liking it I left Canada and came to Southern California. I was a naïve kid then, a classic hayseed farm boy. I felt lost, and I didn't know what I wanted to do.

By chance, Dad was returning home by train after visiting California around that time. On the same train Dad met a former classmate of mine who was returning from taking an X-ray technician course in Southern California. He told Dad it was a good field to go into. Dad recommended I take the course, which I did. I was very grateful to Dad, and that began a strong father/son relationship.

While I was going to Orange Coast College to become an X-ray tech, I was fortunate to stay with my sister and brother-in- law, Amy and Peter Chan. They were newly married at the time, and I must have been a pain in the oshiri (butt). I will always be grateful for their helping me at this time. I'll never be able to repay them for all that they did for me.

I graduated from college and interned at Whittier Presbyterian Hospital for two years as an X-ray tech. When I received my license, I worked at Doctor's Hospital in LA, where I met a licensed vocational nurse named Marion Parker. We married and had a daughter, Natasha. I later worked in an industrial clinic for 10 years. During this time I attended college to become a Physician's Assistant. Upon graduating and obtaining my license, I began working at an industrial clinic in Huntington Park, California. After 11 years of marriage Marion and I divorced.

Later I had a dramatic change in my life. The best thing that could have happened to me did. I met Beverly Benetti, a physical thera-pist working at LA County Hospital. We married in 1979 and moved to Claremont, CA, continuing to commute to and work in LA.

At this point I want to comment that after Dad passed away in 1987, Mom lived alone on the farm for seven years. When it was determined that it was no longer safe for her to live alone, wasn't it interesting that although she had other options, she chose to live with Mats and Sumi in Burnaby. She felt very comfortable living with them. Unfortunately, she fell and broke her hip. She was rehabilitated at Holy Family Hospital. When it was necessary to transfer her to a convalescent hospital, again she had options, but she chose one close to Mats and Sumi. She was happy there.

Mats and Sumi would visit her every day. The rest of the family would visit her as much as possible. Mats made her laugh, and in his unassuming way, made her life very comfortable at Fellburn.

He was just that way. He never expected recognition or credit. Thanks, Mats.

In 1989 we moved to Alta Loma, CA where we continue to reside.

Natasha completed college with a major in liberal studies. She married Anthony Bell, and they have two children — Logan, nine, and Ethan, five. The grandkids are a joy and fun to be around. Natasha is continuing her education and has a Masters in Family Counseling. Presently she is interning at a clinic in Pasadena.

Beverly and I continue to work. Bev works full time at County and I continue to work part-time at an industrial clinic. We plan to eventually retire to our condo in Corona, CA, where we plan to grow old together and travel the world.

That's my story and I'm sticking to it.

Postscript

October 2012

Since I last wrote my story, my life has taken an unexpected turn down a different path. I have been diagnosed with pancreatic cancer, which has metastasized to my lungs. Currently, I am receiving chemotherapy and am doing well, leading an active life.

I am grateful for my family's, friends' and everyone's prayers and positive thoughts, which uplifts me and gives me the courage to continue my fight with cancer. I am especially grateful to my wife, Beverly, for her love and strength which has helped me along this long, hard road.

I am looking forward to our upcoming cruise with family members and I am especially looking forward to the next Morisawa family reunion next year. You can count on me being there!

Post postscript

Unfortunately George passed away into the presence of the Lord after a courageous battle with pancreatic cancer on April 15, 2013. He accepted Christ as his Savior and made his peace with God after being angry with God for most of his life. Words cannot express how much we miss our dear brother and our condolences go to his wife, Beverly and his daughter Natasha and family.

We look forward to a reunion with him in Heaven.

Tomiye Lily Mah

(nee Nakata)

born December 25, 1918

Courtesy Family Collection - Lily Nakata in younger days - Victoria

Writing our internment story and family memoirs, I asked cousin Sandi if she could write up something about her mom for me. But Sandi felt this being a Morisawa story, it would be more appropriate for one of us to comment on Auntie Lily from our own perspectives.

While this is not an attempt to write Auntie Lily's life story, I will add a few comments about "Tomichan " — as she has been fondly called by my family. She is my mother's youngest sister and her life has intertwined with ours since we were little.

Just two years ago November on a particularly cold (-2° C), wintry day, I pulled on my warm, hand-knit, pure New Zealand wool sweater. It is deep red with an afghan pattern perfect for wearing on a cold, frosty day. I remember how one day at work one of the nurses had a friend who was selling out her wool shop and brought some skeins in. I loved the red wool and knew who would knit it for me. Sure as anything, Tomichan (Auntie Lily) knitted the sweater, and it was a perfect fit. I still have it after many years.

This brought back memories of how Auntie Lily has been so involved in our lives over the years. Of all my aunts and uncles, Auntie Lily has been the one closest to our family and a family favorite. She and my mother had a special connection with each other in spite of their differences in personality and age. My mother was the oldest child in their family, Auntie Lily, the youngest. My mother was born in BC, was a brat as a child, and was taken to Japan at age 10; Auntie Lily was born in Japan and was a real lady. Interestingly, she came to Canada at age 10, the same age that my mother went to Japan.

When my maternal grandmother returned to Japan in 1918 to help her mother in law she was pregnant with her sixth child. She already had five children born in Canada. They accompanied her to Japan. This child, born in Japan on December 25, 1918 was named Tomiye Lily. She was very much favored due to her birth in Japan.

Her elder siblings (except her brother Yoshio who died in Japan at a very young age and Naoye, her eldest sister) returned to

Canada earlier. By the time Auntie Lily returned to Canada with her mother (my grandmother), Auntie Lily was ten years old. Her siblings, by then were settled on Vancouver Island in Ucluelet and Port Alberni. She and my grandmother settled in Ucluelet with her brother, Uncle Soichi and family.

My parents married and after living in Kelowna, my parents moved to Victoria. There Auntie Lily became extremely helpful to my parents. When my sister Amy was born and later when I was born, Auntie Lily came to help my mother. Often after the fish cannery season was over, she babysat us while my mother went out to work and my father was working out of town.

David remembers Auntie Lily or "Nechan" (big sister), as we often called her, babysitting us. She was usually knitting as we snuggled up to her. She was also with us when the call came to evacuate from the West Coast of BC and she helped us in our packing. By then she was engaged to be married to Ming Mah, her fiancé.

I remember seeing Auntie Lily in the children's cafeteria at Hastings Park. Then when we moved to New Denver, Auntie Lily often visited as she lived nearby. It was good for my mother to have her and the family living in such close proximity to us.

While in New Denver, Auntie Lily took sewing lessons and became a wonderful seamstress and continued to be an avid knitter and crocheter. My sister Amy and I proudly wore the pink and white polka dresses made by Auntie Lily.

Courtesy Family Collection- Diane with Amy and Sumi
wearing their polka dot dresses made by Aunt Lil

After the war was over, she got married to Uncle Ming Mah and moved out to Vancouver. The only Christmas gifts we ever got when we were still in the interior were the ones she sent us. We excitedly opened them before Christmas.

While in Silverton, when my oldest sister Diane had to move to Vancouver as a pregnant teenager, it was Auntie Lily and Uncle Ming in Vancouver who cared for Diane throughout her pregnancy. Following the birth of Diane's baby, they helped her with the adoption process. They were also very supportive of Diane when she trained as a secretary and later secured a job at CT Takahashi, an import/export company based in Seattle. It was while working at CT, Diane met and married Tom Iwata. Auntie Lily maintained close contact with Diane, Tom, and their family in Seattle over many years until Diane passed away in 2005.

Uncle Ming was also instrumental in helping my father find the property in Surrey to where we eventually moved. Auntie Lily and Uncle Ming and her three children were frequent visitors to our farm in Surrey. They were always nicely dressed in stark contrast to us farm folk, yet Auntie Lily would come with her children, Keith, Sandi and Kirby to help pick berries or plant asparagus — what a job that was! Auntie Lily's biggest help was being my mother's sounding board. Once in a while, my mother would take off after a spat with my father and always went straight to Auntie Lily's place in Vancouver to cool off and get a couple days respite. My mother would then return home in good spirits. How grateful we were that my mother stuck it out through the hard times with my father. I'm sure Auntie Lily played a significant role in helping my mother persevere in her marriage.

Growing up on the farm, we had many get-togethers with the Mah family. In later years, that included out-of-town family visits from Toronto, Ont., Los Angeles, Calif., and Seattle Wash. There were frequent family gatherings with my sister Diane and husband Tom in Seattle. Often those visits included mushroom or huckleberry picking which included Auntie Lily. Another fun get together was catching crabs under the local White Rock pier and later enjoying the delicious catch.

While visiting in California, my mother and Auntie Lily were often taken by my sister Amy and husband Peter to the Las Vegas casinos. There my Auntie Lily and my mother handled the "one armed bandits"-the slot machines, with a passion.

Auntie Lily was always interested in the extended family and attended most of the family weddings. All the nieces and nephews have fond remembrances of "Tomichan"-Auntie Lily.

My husband Mats and I lived in the Mah basement suite when we first got married. Auntie Lily's daughter Sandi was our junior bridesmaid with her first pair of wobbly high heels and pretty dress. I recall Sandi always having pretty new dresses made by her mom for her piano recitals and also Sandi being a tomboy. It was fun watching Sandi play football with her brothers and the neighborhood boys on their front lawn. Sandi often carried a little red square leather purse with her, and hidden inside was her favorite slingshot. Later when Sandi herself got married, our daughter Karen was her flower girl and my husband gave the toast to the bride.

Auntie Lily is a seamstress, knitter and crocheter, to name a few of her talents. When both my girls were little, Auntie crocheted each of them peach colored ponchos which they proudly wore. No one had ponchos quite like theirs. Over the years, Auntie Lily was always crocheting, knitting or sewing something for others. Among other dresses Auntie made was the pale gray, long dress she sewed for my mother to wear at my parents' 50th wedding anniversary. With her wig on my mother looked very elegant at the party.

Courtesy Family Collection- Mom and Dad's 50th Anniversary

Sadly, her husband Uncle Ming passed away in 1983 but the following year, nine of us relatives, including Auntie Lily and her daughter Sandi, took a memorable trip to Japan. What a great time we had joining the large tour group sponsored by the *"Old Goats"* hockey team who played hockey in Japan. Besides touring with the nine relatives on the trip,this gave Auntie Lily and her daughter Sandi an opportunity to visit Auntie's sister, Kimiye and her family in Japan. Another fun trip we had with Auntie Lily was our very first cruise to the Caribbean over Christmas in 1988. 15 relatives celebrated receiving the monetary compensation from the Canadian government for losses experienced during the war evacuation.

Whenever my siblings visit, seeing Auntie Lily is always a priority. At present she is almost 95 years of age. After living in Burnaby for 46 years, Auntie Lily has been living alone in her Port Moody condo for several years. She has does extremely well bowling twice a week and seeing friends and family. While watching TV, she still knits dishcloths to give away, does her daily crosswords, and keeps up with the Blue Jays baseball team, the Canucks hockey team and with hockey in general. Watching sports and Japanese television helps occupy her time. With her alert mind, her hair and makeup always done, and her clothes nicely color-coordinated, she is a role model to all of us.

Auntie Lily's biggest joys are her family, the grandchildren and the three great grandchildren. She counts herself blessed. Thank you, Tomichan, not just for what you have done for the Morisawa family but for what you mean to me and my siblings.

This write up only covers Auntie Lily from my (Sumi's) perspective, but I think my siblings will echo my sentiments.

We love you.

The Morisawa family

Post Castlegar Reunion Comments

Castlegar, BC was the site of our second family reunion in July 2009. This was the reunion that encouraged us to remember how Japanese Canadians were uprooted and evacuated from the west coast of British Columbia and to show our families a few of the sites where the Morisawa family and some of our relatives lived. We wanted to pass on the memories and realities of that historic occasion while we *"oldies"* were still alive.

With this in mind, my brother David and his wife Taeko scouted out the Super 8 Motel in Castlegar, BC. What an ideal site it turned out to be. As we entered the door of the motel, we were greeted by shrills of gleeful laughter as kids came slithering down the giant water slide, while parents sat around in the pool trying to catch up with one another. There was much anticipation of the weekend to come as we gathered and chatted at a restaurant that Friday evening. There was so much to look to forward to.

Saturday morning saw us all piling into our cars and following the lead car to begin our tour of the evacuation sites. The cavalcade of 16 cars snaked around the winding mountainous road which brought us to our first stop, Slocan, which was suddenly awakened by this long string of cars in the middle of their tiny town. It was hard to guess whether this little town was accustomed to these intrusions or whether they were hostile. We didn't know how often former evacuees like us visited this town, as there was not a resident to be seen with whom we could consult.

While the children took to the playground like bees to honey and others lined up at the washrooms, we gathered around my brother David, who, with megaphone in hand, shared family recollections about this area we lived in after our internment years in New Denver. Although we lived in Slocan only a year and a half, I did have a few recollections. Gone was the sawmill that sent log booms down the Slocan River and in which my brothers got swept in the currents as they tried to negotiate their row boat passed it. I was glad they survived to tell the story. The old wooden bridge was now replaced by a solid steel one. Across the lake, the forest remained majestically still hiding its own stories, as we recalled crossing the lake to pick pine mushrooms. What secrets and tales those trees must have still hidden among their branches.

Courtesy Private Collection- David Morisawa- Slocan site- recalling memories-2009 Reunion

Also gone was the building that my brother George described as the "*ratty place*" as well as the home of the bullies that lived next door. There was little left of the town we knew as "Slocan".

Before we left, we gathered for a quick photo shoot on the grassy area where those buildings once stood.

Our next stop was Silverton, where we lived alone after Slocan and where our parents and my sister Diane worked up at the Enterprise Mines. My brother Allan lived with them. What fun we had in Silverton looking up our old friends Gordon and Betty Nelson and reminiscing times gone by. We congregated in front of the spot where our old home, the library building, once stood and was now occupied by an RV park. Again memories galore flooded back in my mind. Silverton still had that mining town feel to it. The old hotel, the beer parlor and stores, all refurbished, still sat jealously guarding Main Street. Silverton, still a beautiful spot on the lake, remains an enviable retirement spot.

Courtesy Private Collection-Silverton – 2009- Main Street

Courtesy Private Collection- Silverton- Sumi, David,
Amy, Gordie Nelson, George, Ken- 2009

Courtesy Private Collection- Slocan- Site of "ratty place"-
2009-David, George, Amy, Aunt Lil, Sumi,Ken

Next, picture the 16- car cavalcade winding its way to New Denver, our main tour site.

There remained our beach at Slocan Lake, a grassy playing field and playground adjacent to it. A few remaining shacks housing some permanent residents still stood on the road across from where the sanatorium once stood.

The playground now occupies the site of our house on Marine Drive, one of 275 shacks which stood on the site once called "*The Orchard*" (because it actually was an orchard before the shacks were built on that site). Some old shacks still remained along the road where my Auntie Lily, Grandma Nakata and my Auntie Kimi and Uncle Soichi Nakata, with their two little ones, lived. All evidence of their old abode was gone. They had lived across from the sanitarium, also long gone, and now occupied by the RV Park. This park seemed to be intruding on *our* orchard.

Emotions surfaced as I toured through the few shacks preserved and left exactly as they were by the Nikkei National Heritage Museum.

At the entrance to the museum was a display of the primitive bucket fire brigade. I wondered how effective it was.

Long forgotten memories came to the fore as I toured through the shacks: piling onto my father's bed and listening to him telling us "*ghost*" stories, sitting on the bench with my family eating our meals, doing dishes at the primitive sink. It was hard to imagine all nine of us living in a shack like that with a floor space of about 395 square feet. On display were the kitchen and the living room left intact.

Also on display was the outhouse with the three stalls on each side- one side for women, the other for men.

We then walked through the main hall with dozens of photographs telling the story of the evacuation and internment.

As I noticed pictures of the confiscated boats, cars and bicycles, I strained to look for our wagons, but they were nowhere to be found.

However, some things don't change. As I walked past the RV Park around the bend, the view of the Kokanee Glacier looking down on the lake looked imposing as ever, forever guarding its secrets. As I came upon the beach I smiled quietly to myself remembering the lazy summer days spent on the lakeshore.

After the cavalcade completed the tour through another internment site, Kaslo, there was further reminiscing as we gathered that evening for our banquet back in Castlegar.

The next day my niece Ann Dunphy did a wonderful job organizing the fun events and leading us in the Morisawa Olympics. The children from the winning team proudly displayed their medals! The following acknowledgements aptly describe our reunion experience.

Courtesy Private Collection- Castlegar reunion
2009- one of Mini Olympics games.

A note of thanks from Auntie Lily's family members:

> The reunion last week (July 2009) was such a monumental success, and all of us are grateful for the wonderful memories that you have given us in organizing this Reunion. The Super 8 motel was an excellent choice to base the Reunion and forever etched in memory will be the joyous delight of the younger ones sliding into the pool. Who can forget the Saturday morning caravan when the whole town of Slocan was awakened to witness 16 cars passing through their sleepy town? Who will forget David's personal anecdotes of days past, and forgive us for chuckling when we saw the megaphone, for it was so instrumental in allowing him to share those special memories. Who can forget the wonderful banquet feast, the speeches and the group photo?
>
> The next day, who will forget the family Olympics in which young and old, lean and not so lean, participated?
>
> We have so many memories etched in our minds and in photos. We will remember Claire latching on to Nathan throughout the whole weekend, the fish caught by the kids, the very early morning tee times at the wonderful golf course in Castlegar, the caravan, David's megaphone, the funny hats and Olympic medals, the banquet, and the bar-beque. But most especially, we will never forget the love and spirit we shared with everybody who came, and the contributions from everyone who participated (in large and small ways) to create these memories for us.

A special thank you comes from my family for including us in your reunion. You were all so attentive to mom (Auntie Lily) and she has mentioned to us that she had a wonderful time connecting with each of you throughout the weekend. Let us all hope and pray that we follow the examples set by our parents and measure up to the standards they have shown us.

Roger and Sandi Sasaki and family.

From my brother David and family:

To Everyone:

Thank you all for participating, contributing, volunteering and adding to the success of this Reunion. I am most grateful for not having any injuries, sickness, or accidents during our event, namely the cavalcade of 16 cars making the visiting circuit without incident. In future events, we will ensure there are periodic bathroom stops, as it was trying at times "to hold our water."

Ann, you organized successful fun-and-games which we, young and old, thoroughly enjoyed.

Amy and Peter, we really enjoyed the meals and the picnic, your excellent choice of food — thanks for doing this job, on budget and perfect timing. We were so lucky in securing Pass Creek Park, and our effort together in looking into it.

Thanks to my wife, Taeko for spending time guarding the purses on the picnic table from intruders passing by.

Thanks, Sumi, you did a lot in compiling information about our background and stories of what took place during the internment, which will be in our archives forever. We all had to try hard to recall our memories, dig out pictures, and documents for the presentation, which helped me a lot.

I hope we had enough family information relating to the Second World War relocation scenario, which we thought very important to pass on from generation to generation. Above all, I hope you had fun. The chats, laughter, swimming, golfing, hiking, fishing, side trips and watching the kids enjoy everything from the waterslide to the picnic gave us a treasured time. Thank you so much for giving all of us the true reunion spirit which we thank the Lord for making possible.

David Morisawa

Courtesy Family Collection- Group Photo- Castlegar Reunion- 2009

Afterthoughts

A conspiracy of silence existed for many years and bad memories were repressed or talked about only amongst ourselves. In the last few years we have become more comfortable talking about the internment. Lately the younger generation has expressed great interest in our history and great concern that our stories might follow us to the grave without being acknowledged. They have encouraged us to remember the past and write it down. Because many stories of the internment are surfacing, I have taken this opportunity to write our story.

I remember the summer of 1955, when I visited the agriculture buildings at the PNE that year with my friend and her father. As we walked down a ramp joining one building to another, suddenly, a sense of familiarity struck me. I blurted out, "I used to live here!" My friend and her father remained silent. They seemed to know the truth all too well of how the Japanese Canadians were once housed in those cattle stalls.

Memories of that experience made me realize how little I and my siblings understood the pressures and hardships our parents experienced. For example, it was not until my husband and I excitedly purchased our first home in Burnaby, that the impact of what my parents experienced hit me. We had two daughters just four and two years of age when we moved into our first home. How would we have handled an evacuation? My parents had six children ten years and under when they had their first home confiscated and were forced to evacuate to an unknown destination and an unknown future. I became angry at the injustices my parents suffered.

For years, this anger at what the government did to my family and my people and anger at Japan's role in the war, simmered deep down within me. I didn't want to be identified as being Japanese. I tried to be as Canadian as possible and blend in as much as possible to avoid being discriminated. This was not difficult to do as the agenda of the Canadian government was to force a dispersal of our community across Canada which took place after the war.[12] When my family and I moved back out to the coast, my siblings and I were the only Japanese Canadians in our school. There were several Japanese Canadians families scattered here and there in Surrey but none in our immediate neighborhood.

For years and years even after I was married, I felt too ashamed and humiliated to talk about the injustice and indignity of living in the animal stalls of Hastings Park and ensuing internment. Then one Christmas the story of Jesus being born in a manger came alive to me in a new way. Jesus, the King of Kings, was born in an animal stall and was also subjected to the shame and indignity of being placed in a smelly environment surrounded by animals. He went on to suffer further indignity and humiliation as He was falsely accused, mocked, tried and was crucified on a cross. Jesus understood my feelings of shame and rejection. He identified with me and others who experienced the same shame and understood what happened to us. Jesus forgave those who sinned against Him

---

12 Hickman, Pamela & Masako Fukawa, *Righting Canada's Wrongs: Japanese Canadian Internment in the Second World War.* Toronto: James Lorimer & Company Ltd., 2011

as He died on the cross and rose again. That thought gave me great comfort and healing.

Being bitter or resentful toward the government of Canada or Japan was not worth the cost of not having peace within my heart. So in spite of the racism and the complete discrimination which was leveled against us at the time, I knew I needed to make a personal decision to forgive those who were involved in the past wrongs. When I did, knowing that God was and is in control of all events and that God will ultimately be the one to bring justice out of injustice, I found comfort and peace.

I appreciate what our parents experienced and the blessings of being a family. Because of my parents' courage, determination, and stick-to-itiveness, and in spite of all their warts, pimples, and wrinkles, they left us a wonderful legacy that underlined their deep love for us. My siblings and I are so proud of our parents who as full-fledged Canadians and property owners, lived as hard working, law abiding citizens (they were finally granted voting rights in 1949). They never had to depend on handouts from the government. They taught us to take our hardships in stride, carry on with our lives, and try not to do anything that will cause discrimination. They taught us to dig in our heels and be determined to be good Canadian citizens.

Like many of my parent's generation, the Issei would be pleased to see that attitudes are slowly changing. Speakers from the Nikkei National Museum often go to local schools in the Vancouver area to share the internment stories with young people. Schools are also invited to bring groups of students to tour the museum to view the pictorial story of the internment.

Many resources are now becoming available to help teachers incorporate the history of the Japanese Canadians in BC into their social studies classes. There are two resource guides made available to schools on the website japanesecanadianhistory.net –"Story of

Japanese Canadians" and "Japanese Canadian Experience" developed by a number of teachers in several school districts.[13]

On the same website under the heading, "Why teach about the Internment of Japanese Canadians?" the developers write:

> *The internment of Japanese Canadians is a black mark on the history of a nation that prides itself on its ethnic diversity, its tolerance and its multicultural policies. A study of the internment of Japanese Canadians raises many questions about human nature, racism, discrimination, social responsibility and government accountability. . . .*
>
> *The internment of the Japanese Canadians was not an accident or a mere coincidence of wartime decisions made under duress or necessity. Life altering decisions were made with little regard to the guilt or innocence of the victims. The individuals who made these decisions were unable or unwilling to assess the issue without bias or prejudice. Many Canadians reacted with indifference and did little to oppose the government.*

In 1988, the National Association of Japanese Canadians, after many, many years of negotiations, meetings, and broken promises from the government, doggedly pursued the Canadian government to grant individuals affected by the internment, monetary settlements, formal acknowledgement and apology for the wrongs committed against the Japanese Canadians during the war.

---

13 Cited from the website japanesecanadianhistory.net. Resource guides-"Story of Japanese Canadians" and "Japanese Canadian Experience" developed by the following: Masako Fukawa, Project Developer; Rick Beardsley- SD #38; Bruce Kiloh- SD #43; Greg Miyanaga- SD#43; Richard Per-SD#41; Susan Nishi- SD#38; Patricia Tanaka- SD#43; Jane Turner- SD#41; Mike Whittingham- SD #38.

I am also thankful for the redress team of Japanese Canadians from the NAJC (National Association of Japanese Canadians) who worked so hard to bring about justice for us. A load of shame and guilt which we as Japanese Canadians carried was taken off our shoulders. Since the apology from the Mulroney's administration, the redress, and the acknowledgment that no wrongs were done by our community, there has been an air of respect shown to us by the public.

A written acknowledgement by the Mulroney government was sent to all the Japanese Canadians receiving the token compensation for wrongs done against them.[14]

I also acknowledge the many members of our Japanese Community who have achieved overwhelming success in their chosen fields and have been honored for their achievements; many have received the Order of Canada for their contributions.

On December 1st, 2012, a small group of Japanese Canadians, including me, who once lived in the barns at Hastings Park, gathered with other interested family and friends at the Dogwood Room at the PNE to commemorate the agricultural buildings as an historic site. Representatives from the City of Vancouver were there to unveil some plaques in honor of the thousands of Japanese Canadians who were housed in those buildings during the war before being sent off to various internment locations in the interior of British Columbia. It was a landmark day for those who had worked hard to achieve the preservation of our history for future generations.

After a few introductions, we trudged off on that cold and windy day through the pouring rain to witness the unveiling of a new plaque placed on a cement pillar in front of one of the agricultural buildings. The plaque memorialized the shameful evacuation event. After visiting another pillar on the grounds

----

14 See appendix 1

commemorating the same event, there was a short reception back at the Dogwood room. Several speakers spoke of their horrific experiences in the cattle stalls of Hastings Park.

My family and I are just another humble ordinary family who walked through a similar journey that started at Hastings Park. Although telling my family story has uncovered some deep, painful memories, I hope it will be a contribution which honors those who persevered and overcame adversity, and that the people involved will be remembered by future generations as examples of fortitude, courage, and perseverance. I have so much for which to be thankful and I, with my siblings, honor and salute my parents for the legacy left for us.

The effects of racism are powerful and creep into every segment of a person's life. My family and I have tried to emphasize the positive and humorous side of our story to help buffer the sting of painful memories and the stigma attached to them which racism has brought.

My family and I share brother Ken's thoughts he expressed before the reunion:

> I think the real story of the internment is how our parents and the J-C community coped with the shock and disruption to their lives i.e. the loss of virtually all their property, their freedom, their citizenship, and their treatment as "enemy aliens." As we visit the site we should remember and pay tribute to our parents and others for their courage, perseverance, and determination that they would overcome this period of adversity. Their hard work and sacrifice have been a great example to all of us and have certainly contributed to everything we have today.

The philosophy of "*Shikataganai- It can't be helped*," so therefore, one must persevere "ganbaru" has also been instrumental in helping my family and the Japanese Canadian community in overcoming this period of adversity. It also enabled them to endure the pain, sorrow, shame and mental anguish with much courage.

For me personally, "Shikataganai" and "Ganbaru" are deeply meaningful and have helped me to cope with what I endured to some degree, but I wish to share that it is my faith in Jesus Christ that has brought me to a place of forgiveness, peace, and freedom. In the end, I am one small voice proclaiming that a Holy Sovereign God is present and that this eternal reality can bring one beyond the feeling of "SHIKATAGANAI- It can't be helped."

I know in Christ alone there is true fulfillment, true equality and true peace. He is the One who brings love, security and significance in life. Ultimately, it is He who has taught me to forgive and helped me to overcome my feelings of shame and humiliation as conveyed in the following verse from Scripture.

> Psalm 46:1 says, "God is our Refuge and Strength, an ever present help in time of trouble."

Bibliography

Hickman, Pamela & Masako Fukawa. *Righting Canada's Wrongs: Japanese Canadian Internment in the Second World War.* Toronto: James Lorimer & Company Ltd., 2011.

Japanese Internment: Banished and Beyond Tears- website- James H. Marsh, Editor Emeritus- The Canadian Encyclopedia. Website: japanesecanadianhistory.net

Kogawa, Joy. *Obasan-* Lester and Orpen Denys Publishing, 1981

    - : *Itsuka-* Penguin Books, Toronto, Ont. 1992

Murakami, Rose. *Ganbaru: the Murakami Family of Salt Spring Island,* Salt Spring Island, BC: Japanese Garden Society of Salt Spring Island, 1992).

Nakano, Takao & Leatrice Wilson Chan, *Within the Barbed Wire Fence-* James Lorimer &Company Ltd., 2012

Ontario Tottori Ken Jin Kai, Tracing our Heritage to Tottori Ken Japan-2010

Shimizu, Dr. Henry- Images of Internment (Victoria BC: Tri- Jean Press 2008), ix

Yamagishi, N. Rochelle. *Japanese Canadian Journey.* Victoria, BC: Trafford Publishing, 2010.

Appendix

As a people, Canadians commit themselves to the creation of a society that ensures justice and equality for all, regardless of race or ethnic origin.

During and after World War 11, Canadians of Japanese ancestry, the majority of whom were citizens, suffered unprecedented actions taken by the government of Canada against their community.

Despite perceived military necessities at the time, the forced removal and internment of Japanese Canadians during World War 11 and their deportation and expulsion following the war was unjust. In retrospect, government policies of disenfranchisement, detention, confiscation and sale of private and community property, expulsion, deportation and restriction of movement, which continued after the war, were influenced by discriminatory attitudes. Japanese Canadians who were interned had their property liquidated and the proceeds were used to pay for their own internment.

The acknowledgement of these injustices serves notice to all Canadians that the excesses of the past are condemned and that the principles of justice and equality in Canada are reaffirmed.

Therefore, The Government of Canada, on behalf of all Canadians, does hereby:

Acknowledge that the treatment of Japanese Canadians during and after World War 11 was unjust and violated principles of human rights as they are understood today;

Pledge to ensure, to the full extent that its powers allow, that such events will not happen again; and

Recognize with great respect, the fortitude and determination of Japanese Canadians who, despite great stress and hardship, retain their commitment and loyalty to Canada and contribute so richly to the development of the Canadian nation.

Brian Mulroney,
Prime Minister of Canada

About the Author

Sumi Kinoshita is a retired public health nurse. A second-generation Canadian, she was born in Victoria, BC in 1938. In 1942, when all people of Japanese ancestry became "enemy aliens" in Canada, her family was forced to move to the interior of British Columbia.

Now a widow, Mrs. Kinoshita lives in Coquitlam, BC and has two daughters and five grandchildren. The story, *Shikataganai*, was born out of a heartfelt desire to record her family story for future generations.

CPSIA information can be obtained at www.ICGtesting.com
Printed in the USA
LVOW06s1109030614

388271LV00001B/7/P